Octavius Brooks Frothingham

The religion of humanity

Octavius Brooks Frothingham

The religion of humanity

ISBN/EAN: 9783743300118

Manufactured in Europe, USA, Canada, Australia, Japa

Cover: Foto ©ninafisch / pixelio.de

Manufactured and distributed by brebook publishing software
(www.brebook.com)

Octavius Brooks Frothingham

The religion of humanity

RELIGION OF HUMANITY.

BY

O. B. FROTHINGHAM.

NEW YORK:
DAVID G. FRANCIS.
17 Astor Place.
1873.

CONTENTS.

THE

RELIGION OF HUMANITY.

I.

TENDENCIES.

IT is admitted truth now, that the thought of a period represents the life of the period, and affects that life by its reaction on it; and therefore he who would move strongly straightforward must move with its providential current. It is not ours to remould the age, to recast it, to regenerate it, to cross it or struggle with it, but to penetrate its meaning, enter into its temper, sympathize with its hopes, blend with its endeavors, helping it by helping its development and saving it by fostering the best elements of its growth. The interior spirit of any age is the spirit of God; and no faith can be living that has that spirit against it; no Church can be strong except in that alliance. The life of the time appoints the

creed of the time and modifies the establishment
of the time.

Among those who are counted prophets in the
new dispensation, none is greater than Chemistry.
It is a Natural Science, taking Nature in its
largest sense. For while in the lower material
sphere it pulverizes the solid substances of the
earth—reduces adamant to vapor, and behind the
vapor touches the imponderable creative and regenerating forces —in the upper intellectual sphere
it grinds to powder the mountainous institutions
of man, resolves establishments into ideas, and
behind the bodiless thought feels the movement
of that Universal Mind whose action men call
the Holy Spirit.

Our generation is distinguished above preceding generations by its instinctive faith in this discovery, and by its persistent efforts to avail itself
of these fine vital forces. Not precisely a *return*
to Nature, for we never went to her, but an *ap-*
proach to Nature, is the general tendency of
things. Faith in natural powers is the modern
faith—often unconfessed, sometimes disavowed,
not seldom indignantly rejected, but constant
still—the only constant faith. Medicine says,
" Lend the physical system a helping hand, and
if cure is possible it will cure itself. Open
door and window; gratify the love for light and
air; put Dr. Sangrado out of doors; get rid of

splint and bandage as soon as you can, that the joint may regain its own suppleness and the spiculæ of the bone may work themselves into their own places; water the physic and reduce drugs to a minimum; meddle not with the recuperative forces of the body."

In Education the new method consults the aptitudes of the mind, humors the natural bent of the genius, and tries to charm the faculties into exercise. The very word *education*—the mind's leading out, as into fresh fields and pastures new—in place of the old word, *instruction*—the mind's walling in, as with brick and stone—tells the whole story of our progress in this direction.

In Social Science the popular theories favor the largest play of the social forces—the most unrestricted intercourse, the most cordial concurrence among men, free competition, free trade, free government, free action of the people in their own affairs—the voluntary system. The community, it is felt, has a self-regulating power, which must not be obstructed by toll-gates, or diminished by friction, or fretted away by the impertinent interference of officials. Ports must be open, custom-houses shut; over-legislation is the bane.

In the training of the young the doctrine comes into fair repute at last, that the disposition must be a natural growth, not a manufactured article; that each character has its own proper style, which must be considered, its own law of development, which must be consulted. If you have a lily in your garden you will not deal with it as you would with a sun-flower. The old system decreed uniformity, repression, the same treatment for every individual, and that a harsh one. Eradicate the special taste; shock the natural sensibilities; cross the working of the spontaneous being; break the disposition in. Now we consult our children's dispositions, favor them and work with them as much as possible, substitute encouragement for rebukes and love for law. If the child goes wrong we throw the blame not on its nature, but on something by which its nature is limited, fretted and hampered. We do not know what it needs, or knowing, cannot supply it. The child is to be pitied for the misfortunes of its parentage or its environment, not punished for its depravity. Solomon's rod is burned to ashes.

In the discipline of personal character, again, the great mark of our generation is a deep faith in the soul's power to take care of itself, and a desire that it may exercise that power to the utmost. The curer of souls learns a lesson from the physician of the body. Formerly, was one tormented by a doubt, he stopped thinking; now, he thinks harder. Formerly, was one saddened by a disbelief, he shut the skeleton in a closet under lock and key, and made useless from the haunting horror some of the most capacious chambers of his mind; now, he drags it out into the day, and sees it decompose under the action of the light and air. Formerly, had one a sorrow, he rushed into his private room, darkened the windows, abstained from food, dressed in black, refused to see his friends, stocked his mind with melancholy thoughts, cherished repining, swallowed cup after cup of his own tears, and by blunting every natural instinct fancied he could, with the aid of a ghostly man, obtain supernatural grace; now, he takes more than common pains to keep his mind wholesome; he seeks the breeze and the sunshine, travels, calls in his friends, reads cheerful books, collects the most brilliant pieces of thought, opens his heart to the dayspring, sets himself some loving task that will make the fountains of charity and duty flow, would rather not see the priest unless the priest can meet him, man-fashion, and give him, instead of ghostly consolations, the honest sympathy of a brave and hopeful heart. Formerly, was one afflicted with remorse of conscience, he stopped all the passages of self-recovery, sealed every fountain of joy, and set himself to brooding with all his might on hell and the judgment; if a cheerful view of his case came up, he shut his eyes, that he might not see it; if one suggested that he was not quite so bad as he seemed, he exclaimed, "Get thee behind me, Satan, with your intimations that I am not hell-begotten and hell-doomed;" if a gleam of hope in regard to the future found its way to him through a chink in the shutter, he stuffed cotton in the chink; he made it his business to muse on his sin to vilify his nature, to anticipate his ruin, to drape his Deity in black. Now, if one has a sin, he does his best to forget it, to outgrow it, to cover it up with new and better life; he adopts a wholesome moral diet, and keeps his conscience in robust condition. The tacit assumption is that men forgive themselves, and are by men and God forgiven, when they rally to do better. So they put *heaven* before them in place of *hell*, and use their fault as a spur, not as a clog. Away with fears! away with despairs! away with devils! away with perdition! away with doom! "In the name of Jesus of Nazareth, rise, take up thy bed, and walk!"

This familiar faith in the recuperative forces of Nature, and the regenerating power of the organic elements of the human constitution, holding thus in the highest departments of the mind, is disintegrating the old beliefs of mankind. The primeval faiths are decomposing under the chemical influence of this quick and subtile Naturalism. Walking the other day through a Roman Catholic convent with a priest of the New Catholic Church —the Catholic Church of Young America—I spied a confessional in a corner of the chapel. So, I said to my companion, the New Church keeps the old box. " Oh yes," he solemnly replied ; " oh yes, there is great significance in that. There a man kneels face to face before the majesty of his conscience, and owns up squarely to his wrong-doing. It is a manly thing to do, and an education in manliness." Not a word about confession as a sacrament ; not a word about penance or priestly absolution ; not a word about supernatural aid ; not an idea suggested that might not suggest itself to a Protestant of the most heretical school. I seemed to see the old Mephistopheles sitting in the confessor's robes, behind the grate, and listening with a leer to the penitent's guilty tale.

Protestantism has the poison in its heart. Dr. Bushnell complacently merges the supernatural in the natural, thus making over to natural causes the work of grace; and then, by deifying the *Will*, tries to reinstate the supernatural in the flesh. But while he carefully keeps open that little over-grown postern-gate for the lurking Deity, he does not perceive that through every door and window the Prince of this world marches in with his legion, and takes possession of the whole theological castle. The old flag may fly from the walls, but the guards are slain and the citadel is in possession of the foe. Regeneration resolves itself straightway into Christian nurture, and the scheme of salvation is a process of home training.

From our own Liberal Theology, the elements of unnaturalism, preternaturalism, supranaturalism, have disappeared almost as completely as they have from the systems of Science. Our fathers admitted naturalism into the understanding and the affections, but left the reason, the conscience, and the soul, under the dominion of traditional beliefs and instituted forms. They confessed the divine authority of custom and creed. They inhaled the ecclesiastical spirit and bent the head to the majesty of established law. They wore the clerical dress of the ancient régime. They were conservatives of the existing order of thought and practice. They dreaded impulse, and distrusted intuition, and feared the devouring appetite of the soul. The understanding was permitted to nibble at the Scripture, and the heart was allowed to eat away a portion of the creed; but the core of neither could be touched. Their appeal was to the common persuasions of Christendom, and the appeal conceded the divine character of the main beliefs of the Christian world; antiquity was with them the test of truth; the miracle proved the doctrine; revelation, regeneration, redemption salvation, were still weighty with something like the old accredited sense. Unconscious, as pioneers always are, of the idea involved in their own positions, allowing inconsistent elements to lie side by side among the first principles of its thought; external in its method of viewing truths, empirical in its mode of acquiring spiritual knowledge, dreading individualism, delighting in harmony of usage and form, judging rules of action by their consequences, satisfied with the outward appearances of order and excellence, magnifying good behavior, prophet of the moral and becoming, confessing a radical tendency to evil in man, which called for repression by all the ancient appliances of the criminal code, and made necessary a stringent doctrine of future retribution—the old Unitarian system struggled between the upper and nether millstones of Nature and Grace.

We are far enough from that now; Naturalism has struck into the roots of the mind. One of the most conservative men, occupying a position on the extreme right, writes a book entitled, "Christianity the Religion of Nature." It is becoming a subtile and a deep conviction that the spirit of God has its workings *in and through human nature*. The inspiration of the moral sentiments, the divine character of the heart's affections, the heavenly illumination of the reason, the truth of the soul's intuitions of spiritual things, are taking their place among the axioms of theological thought. The natural in every department quietly usurps the place and function of the supernatural. Revelation is viewed as the disclosure of truth to the active and simple reason; Inspiration as the drawing of a deep breath in the atmosphere of serene ideas; Regeneration as the bursting of the moral consciousness into flower; Salvation as spiritual health and sanity. Miracle is not a suspension or violation of law, but the fulfillment of an untraced law; the doctrine establishes the wonder; the humanity of Christ proves his divinity; the child of human nature is the true son of God; the guarantee of immortality is the feeling of immortal desires; the pledge of the kingdom is the undying hope of the kingdom; all the soul's books are sacred scriptures :

"Out from the heart of Nature rolled
The burdens of the Bible old."

The creeds are man believing; the churches are man organizing his beliefs for work; the liturgies are man praying; the holy books are man recording his experiences; the psalms are man's utterance in words of his pious feelings; the rites and ceremonies are man expressing his feelings in symbols.

The new Liberal Church understands itself, and triumphantly avows what the older Liberal Church sadly suspected. It has a consistent scheme of thought; it goes to the mind for its ideas; it admits the claim of spontaneity ; its method of obtaining truth is rational; the harmony it demands is harmony of principles—the orderly sequence of laws. " Show me *causes*," it cries. " Let me into the motives of things ; for issues and results I care not. Reveal to me the creative powers of goodness—the genesis of all excellence —that I may bring the semblances of goodness to judgment." It is not disintegrating, anarchical, revolutionizing. It simply demands freedom for the individual, and for every part of him—from the part of him that touches the ground to the part of him that touches the heavens ; subjects the ancient order to criticism on the ground that it nurses anarchical tendencies, scouts the notion of inherent evil or sin or depravity, and looks forward with immeasurable hope to the greatening magnificence of the coming time.

The extent to which Liberal Christianity has succumbed to this devouring spirit of Naturalism is indicated forcibly in the part it has played in the social transition in our country. Feeling the pulse of the age in every nerve, having faith in democratic institutions, because it has confidence in the human nature that is in man—the word Liberty always on its lips—thrilling instinctively to the popular tendencies—it was by no accident, or whim, or impulse of circumstance, that it brought the power of the moral sentiment to act

against that institution which set every moral sentiment at defiance, that oldest and most tena-
ciously cherished institution of the earth, strong
in ancient prescription, sanctioned by the authority of the greatest names, hallowed by holy Scriptures, dear to all conservative minds as a piece of
the primitive rock of society. It has been distinguished for the natural earnestness of its protest against that great obstruction to the spontaneous movement and free play of man's organic
powers. It had no words strong enough to enunciate its verdict on that crime against human
nature. In the terrific agitation which inflamed
the southern mind to frenzy, and lashed the
northern mind to indignation—agitation which
from the field of sentiment passed to the field of
party polemics, and from the field of party polemics stepped out at length, armed for deadly
duel, on the plain of war—the liberal faith was
known of all men as bearing a distinguished part.
From Church, and Bible, and Government, and
Society, and Organic Law, its children appealed
directly to natural justice, natural pity, natural
sympathy, assuming that all saving grace was in
the normal man. Its pulpits poured volley after
volley into the consecrated inhumanity, and many
a pulpit lost its brave soldier in the fight; the
preacher abdicating or yielding to expulsion rather
than strike humanity's flag.

I think I am not wrong in saying that no body of men, with such brave, hearty enthusiasm, accepted the civil war, at the first moment, as a struggle for the ultimate rights of universal man, a battle with the barbarism of the past, a life and death conflict between human nature, simple and free, and the unnatural, the preternatural, in the European systems. When others were deploring the sad necessity, and were dreading the disturbance of the old order of things, our young men flung up their caps and hailed the judgment-day with hope. They went into the regiments as army chaplains; they went as privates into the ranks; they took rifle in hand and died at their posts of honor; they worked the associations which were organized for soldiers' relief; they urged the policy of emancipation; they went among the blacks as teachers. Their pulpits were draped with the flag and resounded with war sermons; their vestry-rooms buzzed with the laborers for the Sanitary Commission. They were unwearied in their efforts and indomitable in their faith. They believed in the divine decree of the crisis, and in the divine inspiration of the people. They saw no issue possible but liberty, and liberty was the mend-all and the cure-all—vindicator, consoler, regenerator, savior. They never felt discouragement, save when the cause of liberty trembled in the scale of fortune; and that discouragement could not last, for they devoutly believed that at last servitude and servility must kick the beam. The army of the North was to them the church militant; the leader of the army was the avenging Lord; and the reconstruction of a new order, on the basis of freedom for mankind, was the first installment of the Messianic kingdom.

Here was Naturalism pure and simple. The axioms of the Liberal Faith rushed to their inferences under the logic of events. In this card we showed our whole hand. The sacramental Catholic Church had no interest in the war, and as little, probably, in the destruction of slavery. The aristocratic Episcopal Church was lukewarm. The conservative portion of the Calvinistic Protestant Church could not heartily support a struggle which involved so much of social, moral, and religious radicalism. Some of the honored fathers of the Unitarian Church, not yet drawn into the current of Naturalism, suffered from a divided mind; but young Liberalism, which is Liberalism carrying out its principles, had no misgiving, but welcomed the grapple in the darkness between the old systems and the Word.

And now, assuming the correctness of this description of the spirit and tendency of the time, and of our relation to it, shall we look forward to our immediate future with hope, or with fear?

Is this unquestionable, universal, all-absorbing and overruling tendency to Naturalism, rushing us into the pit, or impelling us toward the kingdom? It is doing one or the other. We are either all wrong or all right. The religious life and the secular life of the community go one way —the way of the *moral* life. If the times are out of joint spiritually they are out of joint politically, socially, and in every other respect.

Of course it is impossible, as yet, to say what are or what are likely to be the results of the tendencies so many dread and so many welcome with delight. They have not yet transpired in history, and are matters thus far, of conjecture merely. But so far as conjecture will go on the trail of a principle, our attitude, as it seems to me, is one of hope. The powers of Nature do their work well, and do it best the more they are emancipated. How self-sufficient is the constitution of things! How cheerful, and reliant, and self-sustaining, the elemental forces! With what matchless ease the organic laws preserve the unbroken order of the world, in the heavens above, the earth beneath, the waters under the earth! How enchanting the rhythm of their movement! What firm and exquisite grace as they urge the successive and infinite changes from the chaos to the cosmos! Unaided by forces outside of themselves, unassisted by the mechanism of rope, wheel, pulley, lever, they wear away primeval rock, lift mountains from their eternal base, convert forests into coal-beds, change gas into granite and granite back again into gas, take the cast-off shells of infusoriæ and metamorphose them into chalk and flint, shift the ocean margins, cut new channels for rivers, push up green continents from the bosom of the deep, and spread fields over the gloomy abyss; replace noxious plants, poisonous insects, destructive animals, with plants, insects, and animals of higher form and greater usefulness. With the sweetest dignity and the most unerring judgment they handle comets, planets, constellations, tossing the golden balls from centre to circumference, and making the empyrean sparkle from bound to bound with the lively play of the flashing suns.

Working thus in the material world, will the same immanent force work nothing in the spiritual? May we confine our conception of Law to the recognized system of the material universe? Must we not suspect at least that the perturbed will, the eccentric desires, the wandering wishes that whirl and flame along the moral empyrean, may also be held in its fine leashes? Creating such beauty in the realm of material nature, will it create none in human nature? Will the irresistible grace which makes the orbs of the solar system dance to their spheral music cause no lyric movement among the members of the human family? Can the fountain-spirit set the springs among the hills flowing toward the sea, and can it not set the springs of love in the heart flowing toward their Infinite Ocean? Can the all-pervading breath alter the composition of the atmospheres, and can it not modify the commingling of the social elements? Can the pitying world spirit drape ruins with ivy and cover stones with moss, and cannot the quick spirit in man grow over a wasted life or adorn with loveliness a hard nature? Can the decomposing forces pulverize Alpine peaks, and yet fail in the attempt to convert a mass of iniquity into vapor that shall vanish away? Can the light touch of the solar ray cause the whole race of flowers to open their eyes to the sun and glitter with the hues of the diamond as they gaze, and will not the inner light in the breast induce men to seek the all-good? Can the sunbeam call the whole animal world into being and create the very civilizations of men, and shall the Sun of Righteousness be powerless to recreate the moral world and call into being the kingdom of God within us? Can the plastic powers of Nature arrange the leaves with mathematical precision on the stem of a plant, change leaf into flower and flower into fruit, and is there no plastic power in the very constitution of man, that can arrange the elements in

human development, and from the raw material
of passion and impulse create the perfect results
of goodness? A singular inconsistency were it
true! That there should be a living God in
stocks and stones and none in hearts and souls—
a living God in the solar system and none in the
social system—a living God in the star-dust and
none in the dust out of which God made man!

No man can read history for other men, but as
I read history it reveals to me the persistent effort
of organic human nature to come at its prerogative of self-government; and a new outbreak of
glory accompanies each new effort. The successive steps in the well-being of man were successive
emancipations of natural power.

The grand moral achievement of Christianity
was the emancipation of human nature from its
terrible Jewish thraldom. Its revelation seems to
have been that men could judge for themselves
what was right—could please God by being true
to themselves—could find the blessed life by returning to the simplicity of little children—and
could bring in the kingdom of heaven by yielding
to the solicitations of kindness. Man greater
than the Sabbath; man greater than the temple;
man greater than the priesthood or the law. The
religion at first was a consecration of nature, the
abolishment of the old oppressive hierarchies, and
a cordial invitation to the heart to make a reli-

gion for itself. Just so far as it was in the deepest and purest sense "natural" religion, just so far as it emancipated the moral forces of humanity—was it quick and quickening. Jesus broke a fetter, and unmanacled man worked his way upward by the use of his hands. Christianity with multitudes stands for liberty of conscience and soul-freedom. It is another name for personal manliness and social justice. In some quarters it is a name for sobriety, temperance, chastity, and the finest physical condition which conformity with the natural laws will produce. It was a branch of the English Episcopal Church that inaugurated *muscular* Christianity, the Christianity of the oar and the foot-ball. The name of Jesus is everywhere spoken in connection with the healthy normal development of mind and heart. The religion is the *emblem*—human nature is the creating power.

We boast of the superiority of Protestantism over Catholicism, as shown in the greater thrift, comfort, intelligence, of Protestant countries. Is it Protestantism as a system of dogmas or of appliances that causes the difference? Is it not human nature, which, under Protestantism, has a better chance? Catholicism fetters it: Protestantism releases it. Catholicism keeps it supine on its back: Protestantism sets it upright upon its feet; and whatever progress it has achieved is due to the excellent use it has made of its locomo-

tive powers. It was not the free Bible that did
the work of grace, but the free mind which set its
busy hands to the task of picking up knowledge
in every field, and very soon read the Bible, and
a great many books besides, in a fashion that
Luther and his friends did not like. The doctrine
of justification by faith caused thick scales to fall
from human eyes; and the eyes, once open, looked
straight into the verities of the moral and spiritual
world. The doctrine of justification had no miraculous property—it was neither microscope nor
telescope; the laws of spiritual optics helped men
to see.

Liberal Christianity takes credit to itself for the
happy influence of its truth on the unfolding of
personal character, the sweetening of domestic
life, the amelioration of the social state, the healing of the bruised and broken heart, the tranquil-
lizing of the death-bed, the beautifying of the immortal hope. It is a great privilege to be able to
associate such rich benefaction with the Liberal
Faith. But the angel who opened Peter's prison
door did not give him the feet to leave the prison.
The angel that rolled the stone from the door of
the sepulchre did not resuscitate the Christ. Liberal Christianity but said to human nature : " Take
up thy bed and walk ;" manage your own economies ; heal your own hurts ; mend your own
fractures ; repair your own losses ; construct your
own scheme of providence ; build your own house

in the skies; work out your own salvation. Liberal Christianity was the first escaped slave establishing an underground railroad for his comrades. It stands for *opportunity*, not for *power*. Its force is the force of its maker, MAN—force greater than was ever manifested before, because it is the force of the *whole* man. The Liberal Faith is better than others, because it allows more latitude than others. It unties more bands, and leaves men foot-loose, to go whithersoever they will. Do they go to perdition? It is our boast that they go to the kingdom.

Human nature, under liberty, will vindicate itself as a divine creation. The freer it is, the more harmonious, orderly, balanced, and beautiful it is. The physical system proves it by the increased vigor and heightened enjoyment of men who obey the laws of their constitution. The intellectual system proves it by the beneficence of knowledge. The social system proves it by the diminishing vice, crime, turpitude, under the voluntary régime—a point which I believe statistics will abundantly establish.

The moral condition of the world proves it. Where conscience is freest it rights the most wrongs, removes the most evils, relieves the most poverty, corrects the most sin.

The spiritual system proves it; for where the soul is freest it frames for itself the noblest, the most encouraging, most beautiful, most earnest faith. The very delusions it is led into, through its inexperience, are full of a fine enthusiasm and a boundless hope. The aberrations of its untried power serve, like Leverrier's planet, to confirm at last the irresistible law of gravitation, which draws all souls to the great centre—God. Its superstitions catch a light from the empyrean, instead of a shadow from the pit. The enormous moral heresies it blunders into have a gleam of splendor and a touch of sanctity in them, which redeems them from turpitude while they last, and quickly rescues them from the grave they menaced. Its daring infidelities burn with an ardor of aspiration which gives them all the air of saving faith, and makes the unbelief which is of nature look more magnificent than the belief which is of grace. Nature's seers, running their eye along the line of the moral law, catch vistas in the future brighter than those were that now are fading from the Old Testament page; and nature's prophets, putting their ear to the ground, hear the murmur of nobler revelations than were ever given to the old oracles now moving their stiffening lips in death. Humanity's heresiarchs are lordlier than inhumanity's priests. The soul's image-breaking is diviner than the prelate's worship. Knowledge distances faith. Human solidarity more than makes good the Catholic's communion. The revelation of universal Law makes the belief in miracle seem atheistical; and the irresistible grace of the spirit that lives and moves and discloses its being in humanity, sweeps past the dispensations of Catholic and Protestant Christendom, as the eagle distances the dove.

It is not to be denied that our position is beset with many perplexities, and that, as thinkers, we take our chance with the rest, who are seekers in the domain of positive knowledge. We discredit theology; we have conceived a distrust of system; we put not our faith in metaphysics. If we are to have a philosophy of the universe we must find a new one; we must begin again; we must wait. The former things have passed away. The theological system of the old world is not for us under any guise. The spirit of it has fled. The virtue has departed from its sacraments, the meaning from its symbols, the sense from its formulas. Our bark has sunk to another sea, and speeds before other gales to another harbor. If the sea is not always smooth, or the gale always steady, or the harbor always in full view, as much may be said of every sea, of every gale, of every harbor which the ship of our humanity tries.

II

GOD.

OURS is an age of restatements and recon-
structions, of conversions and "new departures," in many directions. There is an un-
easy feeling in regard to the foundations of belief.
The old foundations have been sorely shaken.
The structure still stands, and presents a fine
appearance; but the ground is settling, and the
walls show signs of weakness. There is not a
single cardinal doctrine of Romanist or Protestant
theology that has not been so far qualified as to be
virtually rejected by some leading teacher; so
that, taking these teachers collectively, it may be
said that the whole system of so-called "Christianity" has been abandoned by its own defenders.
It presents a sound aspect still, and will present a
brave front for generations yet to come. It has
antiquity in its favor; it is rich, famous, powerful
in prestige, thoroughly organized, with perfect
machinery in fine condition. It still draws the
people by force of association and habit, by the
allurements of art, the fascinations of beauty, the

seductions of personal interest and fashion, the dignified attractions of historic renown, and the questionable wiles of social advantage. It holds the keys of patronage, and commands the approaches to influence and distinction. It is flourishing in the branches, but it is dying at the root. It does not engage the living thought or possess the moral sympathy of the time. Neither the intellect, nor the conscience, nor the earnest feeling of the modern world confesses allegiance to it. The intellect is busy with other problems than those it propounds. The conscience is about other tasks than those it appoints. The heart is indebted to it neither for the burning of its hope nor the trembling of its fear; it neither goes to it for its consolation nor blesses it for its peace. One summer night the inhabitants of a country house were startled from sleep by a crash of thunder which told them a bolt had fallen in the immediate neighborhood of their dwelling. In the morning search was made for the ruin, but none was found. The out-buildings were not harmed; the trees were unscathed; not a bush was torn, not a flower bruised. But in the autumn a flourishing tree that stood on the lawn showed at the top the sere and yellow leaf earlier than usual. In the winter, when all the rest were bare, it stood at no disadvantage; the snow sparkled on its branches, and the wind wailed no more drearily through its leafless twigs. But when the spring returned, and the other trees put on their verdure, the foliage of this one came back late and languidly. In the summer it drooped, and in the autumn it was cut down. The fatal electricity had made a scarcely visible hole in the ground, and sent to its heart the deadly arrow.

The new faith, which, for lack of a better name, we call by the unmeaning title of " Radicalism," is just beginning to formulate itself. It is cautiously feeling after its lines of definition, and timidly staking out the ground of its future temple. It has made some brilliant studies, careful observations, admirable sketches, serviceable drawings, but hesitates as yet to accept, or even to entertain seriously, a plan for its building, lest it should commit itself prematurely to a system it cannot alter. But the impatient people are asking when we mean to present the plan of our edifice, and what it is to be like. It is in the hope of pacifying these inquiries in some degree that we venture on this faint prophecy.

The phrase " Religion of Humanity " has, unfortunately, been associated with the name and philosophy of Auguste Comte, who does not deserve credit for the main ideas it stands for. If the name was of his invention the thing was not. His leading conceptions—of the solidarity of mankind, of the grand man, and immortality in the race—were thrown out several years in advance of him. Comte elaborated them, but, as we believe, corrupted and perverted them ; for his elaboration was artificial, consisting much less in a development of spiritual capacities than in a mechanical arrangement of outward apparatus. It was with him a manufactured system done with malice aforethought. He found no soul in it, and put no soul into it. His spasm of sentimentality gratified itself by constructing this ambitious mausoleum, which was to take the place of the Church of Rome, but it was *church* against *church.* The monarchical and Romanist tendencies which Comte inherited from his parents, and which his manlier intellect rejected, revived in his later years, and reasserted themselves in his scheme of a new religion. The Church of Humanity was modelled in every respect on the Catholic plan. It had its Supreme Head clothed with vast powers, wielding enormous patronage, and nominating his own successor, paid with a salary of twelve thousand dollars, and provided with a residence in Paris. Under him is instituted a hierarchy of priests, also maintained at public expense. Other elements of the Catholic system are prominent ; sacraments, penances, prayers, interdict and excommunication, saints' days and festivals, as numerous as in Italy. It is the Roman Church over again without its theology ; St. Peter's without a saint. It is the mechanism of the old faith without the soul of the new. The despotic character of the mediæval religion was retained; the distinction between the priesthood and the laity; the distinction between the various secular orders; the subjection of woman to man, of the industrial classes to the intellectual, the intellectual to the ecclesiastical. In a word, Comte's Church of Humanity was in every important respect European. France was the holy land. Its chief city was his Rome, Jerusalem, Mecca. The French spirit of imperialism was retained and exaggerated, made more imperial still by placing a positivist pope at the head of all authority and power in state and church. We have neither space nor disposition to give here a critical account of Comte's scientific chimera. These hints of its character are thrown out that the reader may understand why we repudiate it, as we do, and may believe us perfectly sincere in disavowing all purpose of recommending a system which seems to be full of pernicious elements and wholly at variance with the intellectual, social, and spiritual tendencies of the age.

The human mind must interpret the Religion of Humanity in accordance with its own principles of thought and feeling. It must think it out and work it out for itself, availing itself of all good suggestions, eager to learn what has been discovered in regard to its leading principles, gratefully welcoming contributions of doctrine and sentiment from whatever quarter coming, but starting from its own premises, and proceeding along its own lines, consulting its own needs and building to suit its own convenience; not adopting the plan of even the most accomplished foreign architect, but working its problems out after a fashion and towards conclusions of its own.

At the heart of all religions lie certain great ideas which they make it their business to interpret. They are the staple of religious thought. They are not the property of one faith, but are the common property of mankind; no more prominent in one faith than in another, but central in all faiths. Whence they come we know not. They always have been, and they are. Buddha did not invent them, nor Zoroaster. They are not the discovery of Moses or of Jesus. Each found them, took them, used them, built upon them the system that bears his name. These ideas give life to all religious speculation, warmth to all religious feeling. They constitute the framework which the heart and soul clothe with flesh. There has never been a religion without them; it is hard to conceive that there ever should be a religion without them. Science may rule them out of its province, philosophy may decline to deal with them; but religion stakes on them its very existence. It may be that religion will one day decline and pass away, giving place to philosophy and science; but until that day comes they will hold their ancient place and command their ancient respect, exercising thought and feeling and conviction as of old. What are these ideas which science disavows, of which philosophy takes no cognizance, and which religion claims as peculiarly its own ? Here are some of them : God, Revelation, Incarnation, Atonement, Providence, Immortality. There may be others, but these are vital and cardinal. These every religion interprets after its manner, but no religion has authority to interpret them finally, or for any save its own adherents. Christianity offers an interpretation of them—an interpretation that has stood two thousand years, and has gained the assent of the most intelligent portions of mankind—but the interpretation of Christianity is not the sole, authoritative or final one. Though Christianity as a system of faith should pass away, these ideas would remain, to be set in new lights, and loaded with fresh significance. Religions may succeed one another for thousands of years to come, but till the heart that warms them with life grows cold, till the devout affections from which they spring dry up, till awe and reverence and fear and hope and love and aspiration cease, these ideas will excite and charm and exalt, will try the mind and test experience, and sound the deeps of feeling, and put imagination on new quest after the secret of spiritual life.

Let us look at the first-mentioned idea—the

idea of God—by the light of the Religion of Humanity. About a century ago, in France and elsewhere in Europe the belief in God seemed passing away. The very name of God was spoken in derision, as a word that was no longer powerful to conjure by. A philosopher declined an article on God for his encyclopedia, saying the question of God had no significance. He who professed belief in God was black-balled at the clubs. A distinguished American—I think it was Dr. Franklin—remarking in a philosophical company in Paris that he never saw an atheist, and did not believe there was one, a gentleman replied, " Well, you may have that pleasure now. Every man here is an atheist." In fact, for a brief period the belief in God had lost its hold on cultivated minds; materialism had the argument. But since then the ancient conviction has been taking heart, and has steadily pushed its antagonist to the wall. And this in the face of physical science, which has in these latter days attained prodigious growth, and has been sweeping gods and demi-gods out of the world as the house-maid sweeps chips and cobwebs from a parlor. Definitions of God have been vanishing, idols have been tumbling, symbols have been fading away, trinities have been dissolving, personalities have been waning and losing themselves in light or in shadow; but the Being has been steadily coming forward from the background, looming up from the abyss, occupying the vacant spaces, flowing into the dry channels, and taking possession of every inch of matter and mind. The mystery of it deepens, but the conviction of it deepens also. The great John Newman, the English Catholic, says, "Of all points of faith, the being of a God is encompassed with most difficulty and *borne in upon our minds with most power.*" Ernest Renan, to whom the word "religion" means about as little as it does to anybody, writes, in a somewhat similar strain, "Under one form or another, God will always stand for the full expression of our supersensual needs. He will ever be the category of the Ideal, the form under which things eternal and divine are conceived. The word may be a little clumsy, perhaps; it may need to be interpreted in senses more and more refined, but it will never be superseded." Etienne Vacherot, a scholar and a philosopher of the finest intellectual grain, a man of pure intelligence, who believes that religion under every form belongs to the childhood of mankind and is destined to pass away and be supplanted by philosophy, as it is already in educated minds, will not let go the thought of the absolutely perfect Being. Pantheism is to him the last impiety, because it identifies this Being with an imperfect, undeveloped universe, and so drags perfection down to mere conditions. Atheism is intolerable because it abolishes the ideal world altogether, and leaves man nothing to aspire after. The personal God of the theist he will not accept, for He is too much like a man. His deity must be of the most refined intellectuality, the most ethereal texture of spirit; but so far from being unreal or attenuated, he is the most solid and positive entity there is. The avowed atheist—for there are such—finds it harder to put his creed into words and to adjust it to the human mind than ever Athanasius did to define his doctrine of trinity. You cannot push him into a corner; you cannot make him avow his unbelief in unqualified terms; you cannot compel him to back out of the region of confessed divinity. He retires beyond the reach of definition, but not beyond the reach of thought.

Comte says, " The principle of theology is to explain everything by supernatural wills. That principle can never be set aside until we acknowledge the search for *causes* to be beyond our reach, and limit ourselves to the knowledge of *laws.*" And again, " The universal religion adopts as its fundamental dogma the fact of the existence of an order which admits of no variation, and to which all events of every kind are subject. That there is such an order can be

shown as a fact, but it cannot be explained."
How can a man who uses those tremendous
words "law" and "order" hesitate to use the
other tremendous words "cause" and "God?"
What is *law* but steady, continuous, persistent,
consistent power; cumulative, urgent, regulated
power; power moving along even tracks and
pressing towards distinct aims; power with a
past behind it and a future before; power that is
harmonious, rhythmical, as he calls it himself, *orderly?* Can he conceive of such a power as unintelligent? Can he conceive of it as intelligent
and purposeless? Can he conceive of it as pur-
poseful and yet as uncausing? Does not the
very word "force," as science uses it, compel the
association with mind and will? And can we
think of mind and will without thinking with the
same brain-throb of wisdom and goodness? It
seems as if one must have completely suppressed
in his memory the constitution of the human
mind, to help being dragged by such overbearing
words as "law" and "force" and "order," upward out of all the meshes of materialism towards the Infinite and Perfect One. It is logical precision itself that lends wings. The very
stones of fact become ethereal, and float us upon
the eternal sea.

Whither, cries the psalmist, whither shall I go
from thy spirit, whither shall I flee from thy pres-

ence? Whither, indeed! In the metaphysical
as in the physical world the divine Omnipresence
is inevitable. If we ascend up into the thin ether
of thought, there, in the still rarified atmosphere
of ideas, is He. If we make our bed in hell
among coarse conceptions and wild, animal passions, there, among sensualists, scoffers, and blas-
phemers, a dark, shadowy, brooding terror is He.
If we take the wings of the morning and speed
away to the uttermost parts of the sea, there,
among fossil shells and petrified bones, the skel-
etons of monstrous creatures, the hideous wastes
and wildernesses of the pre-adamite world, there,
in the formless void, there, in the writhing convolutions of the cooling fire mist, is He, leading
and holding with his unseen but omnipotent
hand.

But while thus with firm and eager asseveration
we declare that God is, with asseveration equally
firm and resolute we declare that he is unsearchable. This is as truly, as universally, a doctrine
of religion as the other. The old Hebrew Bible
is emphatic on this point: "Canst thou by searching find out God?" "It is high as heaven:
what canst thou do? deeper than hell; what
canst thou know?" "Thy way is in the sea, and
thy path in the great waters: thy footsteps are
not known." The Christian Scriptures echo the
strain: "The Light shone in darkness, and the

darkness comprehended it not." "No man hath seen God at any time." "Eye hath not seen, nor ear heard." Job is dumb, lays his hand on his mouth, and says penitently, "I have spoken what I did not understand, what I did not know." The psalmist exclaims, "Such knowledge is too wonderful for me." The prophet hides his face before the Lord.

Christian teachers have with one voice proclaimed the doctrine of a hidden God. It was the background of every other doctrine. The eloquent language of Hooker embodies in devout and tender phrase the thought of generations of theologians, divines, and mystics : " It is dangerous for the feeble brain of man to wade far into the doings of the Most High, whom, although to know be life, and joy to make mention of his name, yet our soundest knowledge is to know that we know him not as indeed he is, neither can know him, and that our safest eloquence concerning him is our silence, whereby we confess without confession that his glory is inexplicable, his greatness beyond our capacity and reach." Henry Mansell, the champion of the severest orthodoxy, writes, " The conception of the Absolute and Infinite, from whatever side we view it, appears encompassed with contradictions. There is a contradiction in supposing such an object to exist, and there is a contradiction in supposing it not to exist. There is a contradiction in conceiving it as one, and there is a contradiction in conceiving it as many. There is a contradiction in conceiving it as personal, and there is a contradiction in conceiving it as impersonal. It cannot, without contradiction, be represented as active, nor, without equal contradiction, be represented as inactive. It cannot be conceived as the sum of all existence; nor yet can it be conceived as a part only of that sum." With equal force and solemnity Herbert Spencer, whom the unreflecting call a foe to religion, writes, " In all directions our investigations bring us face to face with an insoluble enigma; and we ever more clearly perceive it to be an insoluble enigma. We learn at once the greatness and littleness of the human intellect,—its power in dealing with all that comes within the range of experience, its impotence in dealing with all that transcends experience. We realize with a special vividness the utter incomprehensibleness of the simplest fact considered in itself. The scientific man, more truly than any other, *knows* that in its essence nothing can be known." Thus from all sides comes the same confession. Thus in all places we see all sorts of men building altars to the unknown and unknowable God. From the orthodox dogmatist, who affirms that " a God understood would be no God at all," that "to think that God is, as we can think him to be, is blasphemy," to the Unitarian believer, who says, " Until we touch upon the mysterious we are not in contact with religion, nor are any objects reverently regarded by us except such as from their nature or their vastness are felt to transcend our comprehension," the testimony is unanimous.

Every seeker brings back the same report. Science scales all heights and sounds all abysses, counts the stars, turns over the granite leaves of the globe's history, bathes in the light of the morning and broods amid the shadows of the evening, and comes back from ocean caverns and mountain peaks, from beds of fossils, and from the silvery pavement of the milky way, with the same unvarying message : " There are footprints, but He that made them could not be found."

Intellect takes up the quest. The designed shows the Designer. But what does the apparently undesigned show ? The watchmaker makes a watch : but who makes the gold, the platinum, the steel, the diamond ? Who sets on foot the laws that bid its mechanism run ? The watchmaker puts things nicely together : but whence came the things ? Whence came the properties in the metals and springs? Whence came the possibility of their doing anything when put together ? Whence came the watchmaker ? Whence the watchmaker's brain ? Whence the tingling sensation that he calls thought? Again the hand is upon the mouth.

The heart sends out over the waste of waters the dove of its tender feeling; but the wearied wing finds no resting place on the boundless billow. The timid bird hurries back to its home, in its mouth no message, but an olive branch, the symbol of peace.

With sturdy resolution conscience goes forth to sound the dim and perilous way. But the scent is lost amid the jungles and rocky passes of the world. Terrified by the glare of the tiger, the spring of the leopard, the coil of the serpent, the sting of the reptile, horror stricken by triumphant iniquity and bleeding equity, shocked at seeing a Tiberius on the throne and a Jesus on the cross, Nero an emperor and Epictetus a slave, it loses the thread of the moral law, and recoils from problems it cannot confront. With the lamp of duty pressed faithfully against its bosom, it stands with bended head and waits.

Boldest of all, the soul plumes her wings of faith for a flight to the very empyrean itself. Her pinions of aspiration bear her above the earth; she distances vision, outruns the calculations of the mathematician, leaves time and space behind, with open eye looks steadily at the sun. But the sun itself is a shadow. Light there is, a shoreless ocean of light, atmospheres glowing with its radiance, throbbing with its gracious undulations; on its waves she floats serenely; in its silence she rests at peace. But no voice breaks the silence, no form of creative godhead walks on the sea of glory. The soul must be content to find a home as wide as infinite thought, as warm as eternal love; but never to see the fashioner of it, never to find the soft bosom of the mother in whose breast it can nestle. She dwells in a castle of air, built by the vapors exhaled from tears, and made gorgeous by the upward-slanting light of her hope.

But of what possible use can such a God as this be? some will ask. "A hidden God!" "A God unknown and unknowable!" "A God who sends no private message and receives no private audiences!" Against the assertion of the Christian theologian that a God understood would be no God at all is set the protest of the Christian sentimentalist that a God not understood is no God at all.

But the conception of God simply as being, the bare intellectual conception of him—the less definite, in some respects, the better—is of vast moment to the life of mankind.

I. Mentally. The thought that the upper spheres of the world are filled with Mind is of immense value. It spreads a firmament, and gems it with stars. Suppose for a moment that the visible heavens were blotted out; that there was no morning radiance and no evening glow; that no morning or evening star shot its beam out of the twilight; that no planet wandered, and no constellation blazed. To the cultivated man the loss would be immeasurable; but to the boorish man it would be immeasurable, too. Though he knew nothing about the heavens, never saw a telescope, never heard of astronomy, only thought of the morning as calling him to labor, only thought of the evening as permitting him to rest, never gazed with other than blankest wonder at " the majestical arch fretted with golden fires "— still, that all-covering canopy being taken away, that luminous immensity being abolished, that far-off, spreading, encompassing mystery being withdrawn, the rudest mind would be deprived of a sense of grandeur it never accounted for or was conscious of, but never could be quite unimpressed by. The sense of a space overhead peopled with moving though never approaching orbs; the feeling of a fathomless upper world, bright and shadowy by turns, by turns calm and convulsed, lowering with portentous storms and serene with bottomless depths of blue; the field of light, the battle-ground of clouds—could not be taken away without leaving the mind impoverished and depressed.

The Roman poet described the difference between man and the lower creatures by saying, " He gave to man an uplifted countenance, and bade him survey the sky." He was thinking only of the ethereal vault. But let those eternal spaces be thought of as filled with eternal *mind*, and what an expansion the human intelligence receives! Naturalists have accustomed us to look downward for our origin, to trace our ancestry in the ape, and, further back still, in the kangaroo and the crocodile. But if such were our progenitors, the sooner they are forgotten the better. There is small benefit in bathing in primeval oceans, plashing about in preadamite ooze, rehearsing the experiences of the cave and jungle, reproducing the sensations of prehensile claws and caudal extremities. If we cannot deny our ignoble origin, we can at least forbear to speak of it. If we cannot get the baboon out of our blood, we can at least get him out of our imagination. We need not be forever looking into the skeleton pit. Does the lily think of its stem? Does the century-plant draw its glory from its twisted, uncouth stalk? What if we are natural products, shall we never ask for air and light? What if we are plants sucking juices from slimy and most unfragrant compost, will the plant live without atmosphere and sunshine? Will the shrub flourish in a cellar? It requires the upper world for sustenance as much as the lower. The leaves spread out their hands to heaven to catch the descending sunbeam, and open every one of their myriad pores to arrest the passing breath of that spirit which bloweth as it listeth. The mere thought of a supernal intelligence is such a sunbeam. The bare conception of a brooding will is such an atmosphere. The very idea that the source of life is above, and not below, that the creative power *descends* before it *ascends*, that the streams of energy that trickle underground and burst up in springs have their origin in vapors that gather on the invisible, unapproachable summits of the mountains of the dawn, the very imagination of a Being who is a celestial spirit, and not a telluric force or world demon—puts the mind in a noble attitude. If the word " God " did nothing but make us look up, and not down, it would deserve a place in the vocabulary of mankind ; for it would break the tyranny of organization, and would open the " eastern windows of divine surprise."

II. In the next place, the importance of the thought of God, and especially the thought of a hidden God, is of inestimable value to the spiritual nature which aspires, worships, adores. " It is the *glory* of God to conceal a thing," says the wise Solomon. " Verily thou art a God that hidest thyself, O God of Israel, our Saviour !" exclaims the prophet. The woods were God's first temples, because they were full of baffling shadows. The evening hour is the hour of contemplation, for it is the dim, vague, misty time when observation ceases and wonder begins. The imagination lives in the undefined. If we knew all about God we should need another being to adore. If we could see him we should desire to see behind him. The God who is familiar is unimpressive. In China, relates a traveller, " if the people, after long praying to their images, do not obtain what they desire, they turn them off as impotent gods; give them hard names, and heap blows upon them. "How now, dog of a spirit!" they cry; " we give you lodging in a magnificent temple, we gild you handsomely, feed you well, and offer incense to you: yet, after all this care, you are so ungrateful as to refuse us what we ask." Whereupon they fasten cords to him, pull him down, and drag him along the streets, through mud and over dunghills, to punish him for the expense of perfume they have wasted on him. If, in the meantime, it happens that they obtain their request, then, with much ceremony, they wash him clean, carry him back, set him in his niche again, and make excuses for what they have done. " To tell the truth," they say, " we were somewhat too hasty: but what is done cannot be undone. Let us say no more about it: if you will forget what is past, we will gild you over again."

In proportion as they claim to be familiar with their Deity, men become irreverent towards him. Mr. Spurgeon talks with God in prayer as a driving business man in need of a loan talks to a wealthy friend. He seizes the balustrade before him with both hands, and puts his case with a directness that seems quite sure of its object; "We have not much to give you," he says, with honest frankness, "only five barley loaves and a few small fishes, but you can feed us with them." The divine, who understands God's secret purposes, peddles out the mysteries of creation as deftly as the keeper of a booth at a village fair. Here is the prayer of a sainted English divine— he is praying for his two children who are dangerously ill: "If the Lord will be pleased to grant me this my request concerning my children, I will not say as the beggars at our door use to do, 'I'll never ask anything of you again;' but, on the contrary, thou shalt hear oftener from me than ever: and I will love thee better as long as I live." Compare this with the prayer of the theist Socrates: "Grant that I may be inwardly pure and that my lot may be such as shall best agree with a right disposition of the mind." The first is the petition of a man whose God is known; the second, the petition of a man whose God is hid. The first is the supplication of the man who would have God do *his* will; the second is the petition of a man who bows before the divine, inscrutable will. As definition becomes sharp, devoutness disappears. The soul places God in the background of existence, not in the foreground: as the centre of mystery, the quickener of awe and trust, the inspirer and minister of the devout affections, the object towards which faith strains its eye, on which hope leans, beneath which patience sits, as the sum of possibility, the goal of perfection. He is needed *there*. We meet the infinite, as Adam in Eden did, among the shadows at the cool close of the day; as the patriarch did, when the dews were falling and the dusk was creeping on; in the weird eerie hour which belongs neither to the night which is to fold in our unconsciousness, nor to the day that has been guiding our steps,—the hour when little is seen and much suggested, little discovered, but much felt; when palpable objects are becoming dimmer, and the boundless impalpable is becoming each instant more thickly sown with stars.

The most unintelligible sayings about God are the most impressive to the religious mind: "God is spirit;" "In him we live and move and have our being;" "God is a circle whose centre is everywhere, whose circumference is nowhere;" "I am alpha and omega;" "I am the grandsire and preserver of the world; I am the holy one worthy to be known; I am the comforter, the witness, the resting-place, the asylum and the friend ; I am generation and dissolution, the place where all things are deposited, and the inexhaustible seed from which all things spring." A Christian minister found one of his parishioners, in a time of deep bereavement, comforting her heart with the mystical phrases of a pantheistical hymn. The vague words that defied the understanding had an unspeakable charm for the imagination ; she did not want to think ; she did not want to feel ; she wanted to be hushed and quieted, and the soft, fleecy language folded her sore heart about with sweetest consolation.

Humility and meekness and patience are children of the hidden God. The noble dignity of silence and reserve, the calm of the high soul, is from this meditation. To him worship is rendered. In the gracious dusk of his omnipresence the weary heart finds repose. "He is nearer to thee," said the oriental, "than thou art to thyself." "Withdraw both feet, one from this world, the other from the next, and thou art with him." What does such language say to the understanding? Nothing. What does it say to the imagination? Everything.

III. Finally, it is the thought of the hidden God that strengthens. It strengthens because, while it kindles the imagination and exalts sentiment, it leaves will and endeavor free. It gives men free play in the world they live in.   The development of individual character, the progress of society demand this.   The living world of use and knowledge we must have to ourselves.   The world of circumstance and responsibility, of culture and duty, of study and growth, must be ours; ours to investigate and to comprehend; ours to conform to or to force into conformity with ourselves; ours to do battle in, to conquer, to shape; ours as a school of instruction, a laboratory of experiment, a field of toil, a home of affection.   There must be no spot too holy to be trodden, no peak too sacred to be scaled, no depth too awful to sound, no laws too solemn to be questioned, no book too divine to criticise, no institution too venerable to be altered, no creed too full of inspiration to be submitted to the search of reason.   Man must be free, nay, must be compelled to do his own work, without interference from spectres. The intruding God mars his own best creation. If God is at hand to perform our tasks, reform our faults, save us from the consequences of our blunders, moral discipline is at an end.   If He answers questions, human wit will decay.   If He makes laws, judgment will perish.   If He sets boundaries, progress is stopped.   If He writes books, genius is stultified.   If He plants institutions, the organizing power is of no use.   Who will attempt the overthrow of evils that God sends, or the redress of wrongs that He permits, or the correction of abuses that He approves, or the removal of superstitions that He encourages? Enough that He inspires will and braces endeavor and makes glorious the dream of possibility and sets the universe to the music of eternal law. Enough that He is at the centre, that He is the circumference also. The assurance that He is there gives us perfect confidence in the world we live in, a sense of absolute security, a complete faith that nothing can befall amiss to him who obeys the benignant rule of the invisible and eternal, but permanent and immanent Father of the universe

III.

BIBLE.

BIBLE, as everybody knows, means "book." The Bible is the book, the special book, the book of books, the holy or divine book, the revealing word, the book that, in a peculiar manner, discloses the thought and will of Deity.

The idea of revelation is primary in religion. God must reveal himself. It is as necessary as it is that water should flow or light shine or force act. It is the nature of water to flow and light to shine. He cannot remain concealed. Without expression there is no thought. Thought and expression are simultaneous. The divine being and the divine existence cannot be even contemplated separately. To be is to exist. To have life is to impart life. Thus the universe is the embodied thought of the Creator. It is God's frozen breath. "God *said*, 'Let there be light!'" *and light was*. In a flash, thought became speech and speech became fact; the three were one. Creation is the visible demonstration of the Creator. The heavens declare his glory; the firmament showeth the work of his hands. Day shouts tidings of him today; night breathes knowledge of him tonight. There is no articulate speech nor language, their voice is not heard; but their *sound*, their significance, is felt in all the ends of the earth. The dust of the streets illustrates his order; the stones proclaim his law; the flowers preach his beauty; the elements declare the flowing beneficent symmetry of his will; atoms, as well as suns, announce the even equity of his decrees. Tell more than he tells, show more than he shows, give more than he gives, He cannot. To use the expression of Goethe, nature is "the garment we see him by," not the mask that conceals him. Who now questions that the world is animated, quick with living powers, burning with intelligence, glowing with passion, throbbing with emotion, crowded with intentions? Who thinks now of a dead universe, of a mechanical world? The old phrase "inanimate creation" is falling into disuse; for matter itself, iron, rock, diamond, is discovered to have no dead particle, but to be the visionary raiment that clothes for the moment invisible and imponderable force. It is nothing: it only seems to be. How foolish the notion that one can be *imprisoned* in nature! As well talk of being incarcerated in light! Intelligence does not confine, it emancipates.

The old conception of matter as a dull, hard,

stubborn substance, which divine power tried to manipulate, has been dispelled. Chemistry, that searching philosopher, has given us a new one, which Shakespeare seems to have anticipated in the great lines,—

> "And, like the baseless fabric of this vision
> The cloud-capped towers, the gorgeous palaces,
> The solemn temples, the great globe itself,
> Yea, all which it inherit, shall dissolve,
> And, like this insubstantial pageant faded,
> Leave not a wrack behind."

But this symbolic revelation does not satisfy the ordinary, unobservant, undiscerning, unintelligent mind. It requires a sensitive and trained perception, such as only the few possess. It is enough for an Agassiz, a Huxley, a Darwin, or a Spencer. The man of science needs nothing more, for he lives among the living laws; he is conscious every moment of the intimate relation between himself and the subtile forces that weave the investiture of God. His finger is laid on the very pulse of creation. He holds in his hand the connecting threads of the perpetually vital cosmos. Why should he not be satisfied who dwells in the " Real Presence ?"

This revelation is enough for the poet; for the poet's eye sees beauty everywhere. He says, "Not the sun nor the summer, but every hour and season yields its tribute of delight." "In the woods I feel that nothing can befall me in life, no disgrace, no calamity (leaving me my eyes,) which nature cannot repair. Standing on the bare ground, my head bathed by the blithe air and up-lifted into infinite space, all mean egotism van-ishes. I am nothing; I see all; the currents of the universal Being circulate through me. I am the lover of uncontained and immortal beauty; I am part and particle of God." "The active en-chantment reaches my dust; I dilate and conspire with the morning wind." The man who feels thus in the presence of nature needs no other rev-elation. The symbols interpret themselves to his awakened mind.

But this high privilege of discernment is not for the many. To the many nature is a blank. It discloses nothing. Its supreme glories dazzle and overpower. The landscape that enchants a Coleridge, a Shelley, or a Ruskin is too much for the peasant who lives in the midst of it. To the artist and poet Switzerland is full of enchant-ments; it satisfies, exalts, enraptures. But to the habitual dweller in Switzerland, to the native there, the landscape is oppressive and discourag-ing. The Swiss is, perhaps, the least interesting personage in Europe. He blackens in the gloom of his mountains, and is not radiant in their glory. In gorgeous climes the contrast between nature and humanity is painful; the eye is literally blasted by the vision it cannot understand.

Hence the cry heard all over the earth for a spoken voice, an articulate word, a revelation to the ear, a message to the average mind, an intelligible communication which cannot be mistaken. Such a revelation people claim to have in their bibles. Every race above the savage has its bible. Each of the great religions of mankind has its bible. The Chinese pay homage to the wise words of Confucius; the Brahmans prize their Vedas; the Buddhists venerate their Pitikas and many other scriptures in Sanscrit; the Zoroastrians cherish their Avesta; the Scandinavians their Eddas; the Greeks their oracles and the songs of their mighty bards. The books of the Old Testament constitute the bible of the Hebrews; the books of the New Testament constitute the bible of the Christians. To each race and religion its own bible is best, because intelligible to it, most in sympathy with its genius.

These books contain the highest and deepest thoughts respecting man's relations with the Infinite above him, with his fellows around, and with the mystery of his own inward being. There are found the purest expressions of faith and hope, the finest aspirations after truth, the sweetest sentiments of confidence and trust, hymns of praise, proverbs of wisdom, readings of the moral

law, interpretations of providence, studies in the
workings of destiny, rules of worship, directions
for piety, prayers, prophecies, sketches of saintly
character, narratives of holy lives, lessons in devoutness, humility, patience, and charity. They
express the whole upward and inward tendency of
the mind. Nothing has place in them that is not
felt to concern the soul. The Vedas abound, it is
true, in matter so dry and dusty to us that we cannot read it; but it is all important to the Hindoo.
The Old Testament contains long books of dreary
chronicle and fanciful legend, and at least one love
song,—the "Song of Solomon." But the chron-
icles are read as solemn reports of the providence
that works in the history of nations, the legends
are credited with hidden meanings, and the love
song is spiritualized into a holy allegory. The
New Testament contains many things we never
care to read, and it closes with a wild, stormy
book that is anything but edifying to the modern
religious mind. But the allegorical interpretation
glorifies all it touches, and changes the coarse
images into divine symbols. To the believers in a
religion its own bible is inspired, however unin-
spired parts of it may seem to others.

But why should the Christian Bible be limited
to the writings included in the New Testament?
The creative power of the religion was not exhausted, surely, by the first two centuries. These

are the earliest scriptures, but not the deepest nor
the richest. They are the first attempts at expression,—the spiritual primer of the faith, simple, fragmentary, incoherent, with flashes of
splendor, and exquisite touches of beauty, but no
intellectual or spiritual completeness. The genius
of the religion has been gaining in clearness and
fullness as the centuries went by, and out of its
more enlightened mind, its profounder experience,
its wiser heart, its sweeter and more divinely kin-
dled soul, strains have poured so strong and
clear, so sweet and ravishing, so tender and pathetic that, compared with them, the writings of
the New Testament are but as feeble, passionate
utterances of a newly-born soul. If that is justly
to be regarded as the bible of Christendom which
voices Christian thought and feeling in greatest
purity, then other names must stand at the head
of its chapters than those of Paul or James or
John, of Matthew, Mark or Luke, who set down
the thoughts that struggled for utterance in the
excited breasts of the earliest converts. The
scriptures that did full justice to the Christianity
of Palestine and Asia are not an adequate ex-
ponent of the Christianity that has existed in
worlds then undiscovered. We run over the list
of those who have given expression to Christian
sentiments since the apostles fell asleep, and the
religion became detached from the crude elements

that clung to it in its early epochs, and the names call up master minds by the score. Fenelon, Augustine, More, Francis de Sales, Behmen, Tauler, Gerhardt, Swedenborg, Baxter and Brewster, Hall and Fuller and Hooker, Vaughan and Herbert, South, Leighton, Jeremy Taylor, Butler, Sir Thomas Browne, Channing, Dewey, Martineau— where do we find such various, complete, lofty expression of the peculiar sentiments of the Christian faith as these and their brethren in every generation and in every church pour forth? These, and such as these, sounded the spiritual deeps of the faith, developed its thoughts, searched its secrets, tested its capacities, basked in its sunshine, felt the rushing wind of its inspiration, experienced the full measure of its joys. They were preachers, prophets and psalmists indeed, worthy the name. It is but an imperfect bible for Christendom in which the best words of John Bunyan and John Milton, of Henry More and Henry Vaughan, of Ellery Channing and Theodore Parker have no place. It is but an incomplete bible that contains the "Apocalypse" and excludes Dante; that admits the mysticism of John and has no place for the richer mysticism of Tauler and Madame Guion. Bible writers are of no sect. The wind bloweth where it listeth, and wherever it blows it consecrates. The Christian Bible is not finished, nor will it be finished until the

Christian heart ceases to glow with emotion, until the Christian conscience ceases to bear witness to moral truth, until the Christian spirit of aspiration burns low; when its knowledge shall have passed away and its tongues shall have ceased, then, and not until then, will its canon of inspired and inspiring scriptures be closed and sealed, and then the religion will have lost its power to quicken.

But the Bible of Christendom, be it made ever so comprehensive in its way, will not satisfy the wants of humanity. The Religion of Humanity must have a broader one. The conception of a Bible of Humanity has lately been in many minds. In the meetings of the Free Religious Association it has been commended. Friends of the idea on which the Association is founded have made careful studies towards it. One scholar has been toiling long in the library of the British Museum collecting and sifting the materials of which it might be composed. The project, if project it can be called—it is no more as yet than a fancy—contemplates a collection of the pearls of thought from the scriptures of all nations, the classification and arrangement of them, and their publication as a comprehensive Book of the Soul, which shall meet the wants of the large and increasing multitude who need a more copious supply of spiritual food than can be furnished by the religious literature of any people. The idea is exceedingly attractive to the generous minds and hospitable hearts of modern liberals. It is of a piece with the broad thinking, the warm sympathetic feeling, the fervent aspirations after unity that characterize peculiarly the new epoch of faith. It is rational, too ; for if it be once conceded that the bibles of the race are, like their literature, expressions of the human mind in its natural moods, it must follow directly that all these expressions, supposing them to be equally genuine, are of equal validity. If of equal sincerity they are of equal value. No race has the monopoly of religious faith or of religious expression, of aspiration, joy, praise, moral reverence. Emotions of gratitude, virtues of loyalty and truth, graces and patience, meekness, humility, are as respectable and beautiful in Persia as in Palestine, on the plains of India or the steppes of Tartary, as in the fields of Galilee or on the Mount of Olives. Prayer breathed under the shadow of the Himalayas is as venerable and acceptable as prayer breathed under the shadow of Sinai, or beneath the olives of Gethsemane. Religious emotion, however various in mood or complexion, is of essentially the same stuff and uses substantially the same forms of speech. Every living soul touches India and China and Egypt and Judea in the course of its inward experiences, and in hours of devotion finds itself perfectly at home with the devotees, prophets, teachers, saints and sages of every clime and people. The variety of genius and temperament in the several races of mankind, instead of making their spiritual sympathy impracticable, simply makes it rich and enchanting. It enables them to voice all the changes of key in the perpetually varying moods of the soul, to do full justice to every shade of sound, to satisfy the possible hunger of every heart. It is not unreasonable, therefore, but quite the contrary, to meditate the assemblage, on equal terms, of the vital scriptures of all lands. They are peers and they are brothers; though bearing different names, and clothed in different garments of speech, and decorated with different orders of imagery, they are all members of the same royal and priestly family.

Such a conception of the Bible of Humanity has a fine significance, too, in view of that ultimate pacification of religions of which the sanguine dream and for which the enthusiastic hope. The battles of the bibles are the most terrible to contemplate. They are battles of inspiration with itself; the divine word is disputatious and self-contradictory: the Holy Spirit tears and wounds its own heart; God denies his own affirmation, flings defiance into his own face. If we could make the bibles of the world take hands, the worshippers of the bibles would, ere long, drop their swords. Could it once be fairly shown that the texture of sentiment in them all is the same; that when either of them makes its dominant chord ring clear, the others respond by a low murmur or a joyous chime; that the water of life in them sparkles clear as crystal in all their jars, vases, and communion-cups, and that, whatever the shape of the vessel the believer drinks from, he always drinks the same elixir and always experiences the same exhilaration—could this be fairly illustrated, as it would be by a collection of the most expressive texts, the bitter old rivalries of faith would receive a strong rebuke. Zealots could not justify any longer their hateful intolerance. If jealousy and hate continued, they would do it in direct defiance of the authority to which they pretend to bow. People who read the same bible may hate each other, not, however, as readers of the bible. That is the standing argument against their hate; and to that argument hate will sometimes yield. The simultaneous reading of the same bible by all who read any bible at all would, at all events, aid in the establishment of a genuine Truce of God.

To this scheme of a Bible of Humanity it has been objected that bibles cannot be manufactured. True: but *canons of scripture* can be arranged with deliberate selection of materials. This was done in the case of the Hebrew canon by the learned men who decided what writings should be admitted and what excluded. It was done in the case of the Christian canon, the greatest care being taken to cull out from a large mass of literature the books that have been preserved under the name of " New Testament," and to arrange them in order as they stand. It is simply proposed to do the same thing on a more extended scale. Nobody thinks of manufacturing a bible, but only of arranging and classifying one. The materials exist, and only wait to be combined. The bible is written, and only waits for an editor. Nor would the process of selection be difficult but for the immense extent of the literature to be surveyed ; for the crucibles of time have been at work so long that the gold is well separated from the alloy ; the gems are ready polished for the setting.

Still, noble as this conception of a Bible of Humanity is, it fails to meet the full demand of the enlightened mind. And for this reason : The bibles of the world express too exclusively the *technically* religious, the theological attitudes, and devotional moods of the mind. They consist too exclusively of hymns and prayers, of pious allegories and symbols, literal precepts, proverbs, and maxims of duty. They have a peculiar monotony about them which fatigues. Their atmosphere is too highly rarefied for general wholesome breathing. They do not so much bring divine things near as hold them up before the eye, out of the hand's reach. Their lofty tone is discouraging to ordinary emotion, which cannot attempt such ethereal flights, and takes refuge in literatures that live closer down to the ground. A man's bible should be next his heart; so close to his best sentiments that it will put him into immediate relations with divine things, while yet he is sitting at his door. It should be to him the most natural book, not the most unnatural; the easiest, not the most difficult, for him to read; the freshest and sweetest, not the "best preserved" merely; the perennially living, not the "providentially transmitted."

It is an open secret that neither the Old nor the New Testament meets this requirement. Our Bible is much less read than its reputation· would seem to imply, or its place in the regards of Christendom to render imperative. It is more praised than perused, more celebrated than studied. It is diligently circulated; it is conspicuously displayed on ornamental shelves and centre tables; but the familiar converse with it, where the reading is not made a sacred duty, is not common. And the reason is, that the Bible, taken in its own character, is too remote from the natural sympathies of men. It is oriental and mystical. They must "get up" an interest in it which they do not feel and do not know how to cultivate.

But the thoughts of God should not be remote. We need not go to Jerusalem to find them; we need not clothe them in oriental language. Bible thoughts are simply *best* thoughts, and best thoughts may come to the mind when the man is studying, exploring, talking with his neighbors, travelling in Oregon or California, roaming over the fields of history, or spending an hour with his intimate friends. There are books of science that bring the mind into very close proximity to the divine mind, and awaken feelings of the most tender awe and affection. There are books of history that introduce one to the dealings of Providence with human affairs in such a way that intelligence seems to be admitted into the very secrets of the divine arrangements, and the soul is compelled to bow the head and bend the knee as in the presence of the Father who worketh hitherto and always. There are books of biography, Plutarch's Lives, Carlyle's Cromwell, Frederick, Sterling, Lives of Charlotte Brontë, Thomas Arnold, Margaret Fuller, Mrs. Ware, Robert Hall, scores of others, that reach the hidden places of the heart, stir noble emotions, exalt ideals of human character, inspire heroism, deepen charity, kindle aspiration, give new conception of the dignity of duty and the heavenliness of love, and open an entirely new sense of the intimate relations between the divine and the human. There are poems that excite the purest feelings of worship, that make the heart tremble with awe, glow with gratitude, soar with ecstasy, burn with enthusiasm, melt with pity, and throb with joy. There are works of fiction by such men as Richter, Goethe, Victor Hugo, Dickens, Thackeray, Marian Evans, to name none but the best, that are more effective than the Psalms of David, or the idyl of Ruth, or parables from the great Teacher's lips, in engaging interest in the sorrows and joys, the fortunes and misfortunes, the heights and depths, of human life and character.

Why are not books like these worthy of the sacred name of " bible," if they do bible work ? Scriptures there are bearing the names, not of Isaiah, or Solomon, or David, but of Plato, Fichte, Carlyle, Emerson, Spinoza, which rank high in the teaching, consoling, inspiring, illuminating of the race. Shall they be put down as secular and profane because they were not written in Hebrew and composed in Judea ? Shall the soul reject them on the plea that the writings of Moses are older, that the works of Paul have the authentication of the church ?

No one will, I trust, be so absurd as to imagine that we advocate the binding all these books, or a selection of them, together in one big volume, to be called "The Holy Bible of Humanity." Binding books together between pasteboard covers is not necessary to their performance of a very sacred office. They can do their work as well unbound, and even better; for they can be more easily handled. The putting of our common Bible between covers, and calling it the sacred volume, has been productive of great mischief, for it has in a measure helped to take the writings out of the category of literature. By giving the volume a peculiar shape, and stamping on it a peculiar mark, the impression was conveyed that it had a singular character. If the collection were distributed through several volumes, and labelled "Early Hebrew Literature," or "Early Christian Literature," the charm would be broken. It is the unity of the volume that keeps up the illusion of unity in its contents. But all scripture is not in the Bible, —could not be in any printed bible; nor is all that is in the Bible good scripture. We should be thankful to recognize scriptures so many that the thought of binding them up cannot be entertained by the most audacious mechanical arts.

Thus, at all events, one old and pernicious superstition is avoided,—that of reading the whole Bible through as a sacred duty. Our grandfathers did this, and in doing it fancied they had served God well, and earned reward in heaven. At least this can be said, that no man can read the Bible of Humanity through. No one need attempt to deal with it as a pious undertaking, a mental pilgrimage, a piece of devout job-work. The Bible of Humanity is a literature; or, rather, an order, a level, a range, of literature,—the literature of the soul. It is found in strata all over the earth. It crops out everywhere,—in all intellectual formation, in every kind of mental rock. It is known at once by two distinct peculiarities which cannot be mistaken.

I. It meets common and universal wants. That which we call Bible is not for the few, but for the many. It concerns itself with the principles that all acknowledge, with moral laws that all confess themselves bound to obey. They express moods of feeling in which all, under certain circumstances, share; moods of highest feeling which are universal. The Bible, under any view of its comprehensiveness, is not an expression of the wisdom of the worldly wise, whose number is limited; nor of the cultivated, who are necessarily few; nor of the privileged in station, who are a class. It is not a book of the reason, dealing with pure philosophy; nor of the intellect, dealing with physical or metaphysical science; nor of the understanding, dealing with matters of business. It is not a scholar's text-book, if it were the multitude could not read it; nor is it a politician's manual, in that case it would have no meaning for the millions who have no capacity for politics, or no taste for them. It is not a book which may be perused with delight by some particular class of men, antiquarians, for example, historians, poets, or philologists. It is a book of the *heart*, taking the word "heart" in its most comprehensive sense. It is a book of the moral and religious sentiments, which are, and which alone are, universal, the property and the peculiarity of mankind.' The sentiments of adoration, veneration, praise, longing, belong to the race everywhere, not in its superior, but also in its inferior condition. We know them to be the staple of all bibles. So identical are they in substance that the very language in which they clothe themselves is the same. Except for a peculiarity of coloring, due to the stern Hebrew soil from which they spring, the Psalms of David might be read anywhere on the planet. They are read feelingly and responsively in Chicago and San Francisco, at the opposite extremities of the earth. The magnificent hymn of the Greek Cleanthes would not be out of place in the collection of Hebrew songs, less still in the book of Job, or the Old-Testament Apocrypha. The splendid outbursts of Persian adoration would but add to the lustre of the most brilliant passages in the prophets. When from time to time I have read as Sunday lessons extracts from the Scriptures of India, those who suspected that they were not in our Bible never suggested that they were unworthy of being there.

The moral sentiment is still more universal in its reach than the religious, because it comes closer to practical experience. The ten commandments, with a few trifling variations, are written in the sacred codes of the most dissimilar peoples, showing the unity and the ubiquity of the sentiment of duty. All the bibles contain something like a version of the decalogue. Enunciate the " Golden Rule," and echoes come murmuring from the consciences of men round the globe. The sweetest lessons of charity are repeated over and over by Egyptian and Syrian, by European and Asiatic lips. The heart of mankind grows these natural flowers of every conceivable color and form. The principles that constitute the good life are universal. There is but one essential type of the perfect character. Individual traits may be local or national ; qualities are differently emphasized, proportioned, and shaded, but the basis is ever the same.

The literature that is written on the level of these moral and spiritual sentiments is bible literature, human literature, literature of the general heart. No bible is fit to be called such that

can be enjoyed by a single tribe or nation, that
can be outgrown in a hundred or two of years.
If it cannot be translated into many tongues, if
it does not meet a response in a world-wide and
a world-deep experience, if it is not found native
to certain immensely broad strata of human
feeling, then it is not bible, and deserves no place
in biblical literature. Large portions of the Old
Testament are of this character, whole books, in
fact, are there which interest none but antiquarians; whole books are there which do not really
interest so small a class as these. The New Testament comprises much that is incidental and
local, the small concerns of Palestinian or Asiatic communities, trifling matters of dispute,
arguments on questions long forgotten, theories
and discussions that never concerned many and
now concern none, rules of practice that have
become obsolete, maxims of conduct that have
lost their application, letters addressed to some
passing emergency, one poem, the Apocalypse,
that is curious as a piece of literature, but of absolutely no moment, and of even less than none in
a religious point of view, a book that owes its sa-
credness to its unintelligibleness. These are not
genuine bible, and the infrequency with which
they are read, the difficulty of understanding
their meaning, the falling away of sympathy from
their contents, proves by the testimony of the

general instinct that they do not belong to the class of sacred literature. Bibles must answer to universal needs.

II. The other criterion of the genuine bible literature is that it shall communicate moral power. The test of inspiration is the power to inspire. This is the very definition of inspiration given in the so often misquoted text of "Timothy:" "All scripture, given by inspiration of God, is profitable for doctrine, reproof, correction, instruction in righteousness." Which is as much as saying that the scripture which is not profitable for doctrine, reproof, correction, instruction in righteousness, is not given by inspiration of God. The compilers of the New Testament omitted very curious books on the ground that they were not thus profitable. Luther spoke contemptuously of the Epistle of James, calling it "an epistle of straw," because it treated slightingly the doctrine of justification by faith, which was the spiritual battle-cry of the revolt against the Church of Rome. Swedenborg rules out of bible literature the Pauline Epistles on the ground that they are controversial and didactic writings, and contain no hidden spiritual sense. These judgments may both be arbitrary, but the judgment that is not arbitrary is the unconsciously exercised judgment of the great multitude of Christian men and women. Examine, if you have opportunity, the copies of the Bible that are read privately or in the family circle, and see how unerringly the wheat is separated from the chaff. The pencil marks, and the dog's ears, and the prints of fingers are clustered together at the chapters and verses that nourish the heart, fill its emptiness, brace its weakness, solace its loneliness, comfort its sorrow, still the tempest of its grief, exalt its confidence, and brighten its hope. These are the living scriptures, and all the rest are dead.

Tried by this test of power to inspire, what legions of volumes, unrecognized and disavowed by Romanist Council and Protestant Bible Society steal from the alcoves of secular libraries and quietly range themselves in the line of sacred scriptures—treatises of philosophy some of them, immortal dialogues of Plato, discourses of Socrates, poems of Shakespeare, the Brownings, novels like "Adam Bede" and "Romola," which touch the deepest places of the heart. It matters not how the book be called—drama, fiction, epic, ballad, lyric, narrative, biography—if it does this work it is holy. If it inspires, it is inspired : the helping word is the divine word. The portal of the famous Alexandrine library bore, we are told, the inscription, " Medicine for the Mind :" that is what the Bible claims to be. Did these ancients suppose that all books were bibles? Their libraries were not then, like ours, full of cheap rubbish in the shape of paper-covered novels and sentimental verses. Theirs must have been " books that were books." But books that are books are bibles.

Let one who needs the calm of contemplation take up the poems of Emerson or Tennyson, of Browning or Matthew Arnold, and read almost at random, not lightly passing over " In Memoriam," and not failing to read " Rugby Chapel." For the rousing of the moral nature to earnest purpose and resolve, for the awakening from sleep of the sentiments of truth, sincerity, justice, there is nothing so good as the earlier writings of Thomas Carlyle, the " Sartor Resartus," " Chartism," " Past and Present," " Tracts for the Times."

Is a man afflicted with the disease of bigotry, let him trace the progress of religious ideas ; let him muse with Volney over the ruins of the once magnificent House of the Sun at Baalbec ; let him wander with Layard over the mounds beneath which time has buried Nineveh's winged bulls ; let him explore the rock chapels of Hindostan, desolate now for centuries, or stumble about with Stephens among the sacred monuments of Central America, whose history vanished with the race that used them ; let him endeavor to find the venerable beliefs of India and

Egypt, and to unveil the thoughts that were hidden within the world-renowned "mysteries" of Greece; and, seeing how the mightiest priesthoods have passed away, and the creeds of nations been forgotten, he will cease to vex himself about the cobwebs in his neighbor's brain.

Is he, on the other hand, tormented by doubts about Providence, let him take up the narrative of some particular epoch—the story of the Decline of the Roman Empire, the account of the Reformation, of the Thirty Years' War, Carlyle's "History of the French Revolution," and learn from such books that God guides the world with firm hand, always bringing results from causes, and never failing to raise up the right man at the right hour.

Does one need peace of mind, there is the delicious region opened by the writers on natural history, the wonderful economies of trees and plants, the curious structures and habits of animals. Let one visit the Alps with Tyndall, go with Huber among the bees, explore with Mr. White the marvels of the little village of Selborne, and the belief will sweetly steal into his mind that the care which watches over beavers and beetles will not desert him.

For the serious sickness of the mind, for chronic despondency and deep-seated sorrow, fo loneliness and bereavement, nothing is at once so soothing and so stimulating as biography—the lives of great and good men. These are scriptures indeed! See from them how little a space one sorrow makes in life. See scarce a page, perhaps, given to some grief similar to your own, and how triumphantly the life sails on beyond it! You thought the wing was broken : it was but a feather that was bruised. See what life leaves behind it when all is done—a summary of positive facts far out of the regions of sorrow and suffering, linking themselves to the being of the world. Read, you who bear about a life-long burden which you cannot speak of and which no sympathy will aid you to bear—read Talfourd's " Final Memorials of Charles Lamb," and see how sweetly, patiently, thankfully a gentle nature can drink a cup bitterer than death. Who can speak of discouragements and griefs in the presence of a man like Frederick Robertson or a woman like Charlotte Brontë? Who can despair of human nature while reading the biography of Fowell Buxton or of Blanco White or of the Baron Bunsen? Works like these are not numerous, the less, therefore, is the difficulty of finding them when required. They stand out from the mass of ephemeral literature like evergreens amid trees that have dropped their leaves on the ground at the first chill of the autumn. Whole gardens of butterfly literature perish annually as their single season of popularity passes away. Books of mere entertainment, books which give a momentary sensation of pleasure to idle minds, communicating thoughts that engage attention for a few hours, from a few persons; books of luxury; books of amusement; sentimental tales and verses that charm with a pleasing but superficial emotion; books of polemics and passion flutter and buzz for a moment and are forgotten; they neither teach, correct, instruct, nor console: the books that do this are eternal.

When pastor Robinson addressed the Pilgrims, on the eve of their departure in search of religious freedom, he expressed his conviction that more light would break yet out of God's word. It was a great saying for the time. But a greater saying is given to more modern lips, the expression of a faith that more word will bread out of the light, and that this word will be discovered outside of the heathen and christian scriptures, outside of all so-called bibles, in the mass of those noble literatures which at once give expression to the holiest moods of the mind and nourish them.

IV

CHRIST.

THE question for discusion now is that of the Christ; not the Christ of Christianity, that has been talked threadbare, but the Christ of Humanity. God is: that wo hold with supreme conviction as the central truth of all religion. God exists: that, also, we cling to as a pillar of truth. He expresses himself in the marvellous symbolism of the visible universe; nature is his manifestation. He expresses himself in the loftiest products of the human mind; these we call bible, the written word. Further and more completely he expresses himself in the form of living attributes or qualities, in the form of character. He reveals himself in human shape and personality, takes on the aspect of man,—as the theologians say, becomes incarnate; not an articulate word merely, but an organized being. This has always been felt to be the necessary term of the divine manifestation. Humanity is the highest known form of organized existence. The head of the created universe is man; the supreme power culminates in him; and the soul of man is his humanity, his pure human quality, not his intellect, his genius, his imagination, but his moral character, the sum of his sentiments, dispositions, purposes, will. The race has demanded a deity with affections; heart and flesh cry out for a living God who sympathizes with human kind, dwells among them, teaches, guides, consoles them, bears their burdens, shares their sufferings, heals their diseases, removes their infirmities, blesses them, serves them, forgives their sin, promises them felicity, opens the way for them to paradise; a God who by his teaching confirms truth, by his conduct vindicates justice, by his example shows the intrinsic beauty and the priceless worth of virtue; a God who represents, illustrates, glorifies the traits that belong to all men and women simply as human beings, without regard to condition or endowment; who is not so much *a* man as Man.

Hence the belief in incarnations that prevails and has from time immemorial prevailed wherever men have put their thoughts and feelings into the form of religion. In the imaginative faiths of India, these incarnations were numerous. Every faith has had at least one. Buddha is the Christ, the god-man of Buddhism; Zoroaster and Confucius occupied this place in the systems that bear their names. The Hebrew faith had inspired men, teachers and prophets who came as near being incarnations of Deity as the severe Jehovism of Israel would permit ; Christianity turns to Jesus as its Christ, its Word made flesh, the only begotten of the Father. Even Mohammedanism, that driest of religions, allows Mohammed to occupy a corresponding place in its barren theology..

But this incarnate deity is never regarded as an ordinary man. No single specimen of humanity will represent him. The god-man is always described as prodigious, supra-human, supra-natural, breaking through the confines of individual personality at every point. We read that when Buddha was born, " The Holy King, the Grand Being, turning his eyes towards the East, regarded the vast host of angels, Brahmas and Devas, Yom and Yakhas, Asuras, Gandharvas, Suparnas, Garudas and men ; and they rained flowers and offerings upon him and bowed in adoration, praising him and crying, ' Behold the Excellent Lord to whom none can be compared, to whom there is none superior.' Then, in order, he turned to the other points of the compass, and from each received the same adoration ; having thus regarded the whole circle of the heavens, he turned to the north, and, gravely marching seven paces, his voice burst forth in the glorious words : ' I am the greatest being in the world, excelling all in the world. There is none superior to me, there is none equal to me. This is my last generation. For me there will be no future birth into the world.' Then the ten thousand worlds quaked, the universe was illumined with an exceeding bright light," etc. The story of Zoroaster is made up of similar marvels. Of the prosaic Confucius it is written by an ardent disciple ; " He may be compared to heaven and earth in their support- ing and containing, their overshadowing and cur- taining all things ; he may be compared to the four seasons in their alternating progress, to the sun and moon in their successive shining. He is the equal of Heaven. Call him the ideal man, how earnest is he ! Call him an abyss, how deep ! Call him heaven, how vast ! " The legends say that in the night when Mohammed came into the world, seventy thousand palaces of rubies and seventy thousand palaces of pearls were built in paradise. A light whose resplendence glorified all Arabia issued with him from his mother's bosom. When he was three years old, two angels opened his side, took out his heart, pressed from it the black drops of sin, and set within him the light of prophecy. Mohammed saw before and behind ; his saliva sweetened the brine of the ocean ; his drops of sweat were like pearls ; his body cast no shadow in moonlight or sunshine ; no insect approached his person. It is related of Jesus that he was born of a virgin ; a star leaves its station in the heavens to indicate his birthplace ; kings lay gifts at his feet ; angels tell the news to shepherds, filling the air with their songs and making the wintry moonlight glisten with their shining wings. The pole of heaven stood still, says an Apocryphal writing, the birds shuddered ; sheep in the pasture stopped ; all movements in men and beasts were arrested. Before the wondrous infant, domestic cattle and wild beasts fell down and worshipped ; trees bowed their fruit-laden tops ; idols tumbled from their pedestals ; robbers took to flight ; malignant things were innocent ; the laws of space and time were suspended for his convenience ; The God-man was not to be thought of as an ordinary mortal. He was immense, enormous ; out of all proportion to the rest of his kind. If you attempt to pour the ocean into a vessel, you must make the vessel large.

Look at the attributes of the Christ of our theologians. He is described as eternal, omnipresent, omniscient, omnipotent, unchangeable, sinless ; he is an object of worship, superior to men and angels. He is, though not in the supreme sense, creator and preserver of the world, of the spiritual world the highest Lord ; lifegiver, mediator, priest, saviour, bestower of blessings, forgiver of sins, final judge and rewarder. He is called Son of God, equal with God, divine. He is all but confounded with the infinite and absolute Being. The ingenuity of thought has been tasked to the utmost to state the distinction between him and the Father.

That this language describes no historical person should not need to be said. No individual who ever lived, or ever will live, fills out the measure of this portraiture. Jesus certainly did not. His life was that of a simply human being; his historical career was natural; his character abounded in deliciously human traits; he was subject to physical infirmities, hunger, thirst, fatigue; he professed ignorance on critical occasions; he showed himself unacquainted with matters that enlightened men of his generation knew; his predictions did not all come to pass; he suffered in his mind and feelings; he was often lonely and depressed; he sought the calm of solitude; he prayed with an evident sense of need; he lived much in his affections, resting in the love of very inferior men and women; he shrunk from death and wrestled with the agony of it so fearfully that his sweat is described as big with drops of blood.

The attempt to put Jesus and the Christ together has been made with distinguished ability and desperate persistency, but it never succeeded. By keeping the weak points of the argument out of sight, by breaking down the distinctions between the Gospels, and assuming the genuineness of the Gospel of John ; by misreading and misinterpreting texts ; by accepting as true all the wonderful things reported and making them look more wonderful than they are in the narrative ; by surrounding with an atmosphere of mystery points in themselves obvious ; by carrying over to the historical Jesus the impressions that theology had formed of him, and reading his life by the light of pure speculation—in a word, by assuming their whole case as proved, and merely reaffirming it while seeming to demonstrate it, men like Dr. Bushnell and de Pressensé construct a very plausible argument, which crumbles to pieces on the first intelligent perusal of the New Testament. The Christ of the Christian theology is not the Jesus of the Gospels, but a purely ideal person, a conception, an imagination, an intellectual vision, a splendid spiritual dream. The Christ of Paul, who started the conception, was not *a* man, but *the* man, nor *the* man only, but the ideal man, the possible man, the spiritual man, that is the soul of humanity. Goethe says of Shakespeare's Hamlet, " He is an oak-tree planted in a porcelain vase." To try to crowd the attributes of the theological Christ into the personality of the historical Jesus, is to plant a whole forest in a porcelain vase.

Nothing less than all the humanity there is in the race meets the conditions of a doctrine of incarnation. A perfected humanity would not more than express the Absolute in the form of qualities; a perfected humanity, comprising a world of living men and women regenerate and happy; and surely nothing less than all the completed humanity there is will furnish anything approaching to a relatively adequate expression of it. Indeed, when enthusiasts like Mr. Beecher speak of Christ they describe a person who is more than all living men and women put together. Let us say that the Christ of humanity is the *human element in mankind;* not mankind exhaustively considered; not the whole human race, as distinguished from the brute creation, including all who are in the human form; not the unorganized portions of the race, if there be any such; not the insane, or the wholly demoralized and dehumanized, if such there be; but the human portion of mankind, those of whatever nation, clime, fashion of religion or degree of civilization, of whatever personal endowment and social condition, of whatever age, temperament, mingling of disposition, turn of mind, quality of genius, bent of pursuit, who in any degree or after any kind represent the qualities that characterize the social being. As all literature is not bible, but only the literature that somehow bene-

fits the rational man, instructing, inspiring enno-
bling, comforting, resting, recreating, beguiling
him of his cares, strengthening him in good · resolves and gentle feelings, so only that portion of
mankind which is the medium of helpfulness
and blessing can be reckoned as manifesting the
qualities that embody the divine being. I do
not say which these portions are; they are certainly not to be specified by any known titles or
distinctions, they are not to be indicated by any
technical signs. Possibly they include all living,
human creatures; for who will undertake to say
that any single human creature is totally destitute of humanity, that any single human creature is not in some way or degree serviceable
to his kind? I only drop the remark that if
there be any such, the incarnation has not taken
place in them. Jesus put the publicans and
harlots before the scribes and pharisees; Humanity does not exclude them; it excludes none
whom bonds of kindness make part of their
kind. Comte, with the contempt for mankind
that marks his system, says: "Mere digesting
machines are no real part of humanity. You
may reject them and supply their place by animals that lend to man a noble aid. We should
not hesitate to look on many dogs, horses, oxen,
as more estimable than certain men." But I
make no discrimination here. I should be sorry

to think that there were any mere digesting machines; but if there be any, there is no bigotry in declaring them to be no part of humanity, regarded in this noble aspect. That the whole race is not yet humanized, seems plain from the power still possessed by the elements we call inhuman. The kingdom of God is by no means established yet, the " Christ " is not " all in all." Until the diviner forces in mankind shall have brought the less divine up to their level, the incarnation will be incomplete.

Paul talks of " building up the body of Christ," and says, " Ye are the body of Christ, and each one of you is a member." He is addressing those Jews, Greeks, Romans, freedmen, slaves, men and women who are united by faith in Christ : the rest are excluded. They may become members, they have the capacity for membership, but they are none till they share this mystic sympathy; so the religion of humanity says, "Ye are the body of humanity," meaning those whom the human element makes one

Of late years we have been accustomed to think and speak of mankind as one great being. The conception is not new ; two hundred years before Christ, a Roman poet made one of his characters exclaim : "I am a man, and nothing human is foreign to my sympathies," thus acknowledging the common bond of kindness that makes of human kind a fellowship. Two hundred years ago Pascal wrote : " The whole race of man, through all the ages, is to be considered as one man who ever exists and who continually learns." At the close of the last century, Lessing wrote his celebrated essay on the " Education of the Race," and Herder produced his " Outlines of a Philosophy of the History of Man," in which he traced the course of humanity as if it were an individual placed on the earth by an unseen hand, taking on new forms and pursuing new objects as it passes from country to country and from age to age, enlarging its sphere, multiplying its energies and activities, pressing forward to higher and nobler states, and achieving by degrees the victory of truth, beauty, and goodness. The poet sings,—

" For man is one,
And he hath one great heart. 'Tis thus we feel
With a gigantic throb, across the sea,
Each other's rights and wrongs : thus are we men."

But Paul anticipated the whole doctrine in his glorious language addressed to the Corinthian Christians : " As the body is one and hath many members, and all the members of this one body, however many, are one body, so also is the Christ. For by one spirit we are all baptized into one body, whether we be Jews or Gentiles, bond or free. For the body is not one member but many.

If the foot shall say, because I am not the hand I am not of the body, is it therefore not of the body? The eye cannot say to the hand, I have no need of thee; nor the head to the feet, I have no need of you." The great difference between the apostle and ourselves is here : while he makes the bond of union between the members to be faith in the individual Christ, we make it consist in fidelity to the human Christ, to the humanity which *is* the Christ. His Christ was not so much an individual as a community; all Christians composed the organized form. Our Christ is not so much a community as an element that is the soul of many communities.

Humanity thus described is an individual,—just as Paul said that Christendom was an individual. It has a single line of conscious being. It grows; it passes through stages of progress; it matures with time; its faculties increase in power and number; its acquisitions accumulate; it gathers a common fund of knowledge, experience, wisdom, character, as it toils on. It has intelligence, feeling, reverence, duly proportioned and mingled. Its members suffer and enjoy, labor and gain, strive and conquer together as one person. The people actually living on the planet are linked together by tens of thousands of interests of every conceivable kind, from the ordinary material interests that are involved in their physical existence

to the more complex interests implied in the word
"Society," and then again, by interests of a purely
intellectual and spiritual nature, in which they
share as rational, moral, and religious beings, who
desire truth, long for justice and aspire after immortality. They have the same general sentiments, variously colored by locality and climate,
but in no wise essentially differing; mind and
heart are composed of the same stuff. Their
moral constitution is homogeneous; kindness
everywhere is kindness, justice is justice, honor is
honor, and love is love. The grand beliefs are
substantially the same from age to age. The
common humanity declares its presence and power
in innumerable forms of mutual pitifulness and
help, in great waves of compassion rolling across
the civilized world toward some distressed point,
as Chicago or Crete or Persia, in an immense
feeling of responsibility which has a seat in every
conscience and rivets every soul to every other
soul.

The unity is organic and vital. It holds the
morally living together; it connects the living
with the generations of the dead who have left
their deposits of power in the multiplied æons
that have gone, and with the generations of the
yet unborn, who in the long ages to come shall
enter upon, continue and complete the labors undertaken. The toils, the rewards, the conquests

are partaken by all alike. Other men labored, we
enter into their labors; we labor, others shall
enter into ours. Every gift is common.

The conception of this unity is as distinct as
was that of Paul when he spoke of the one body
in Christ of which all believing souls were members. It is as distinct as is the conception of the
Roman Catholic Church, which contains the utmost diversity of conditions, gifts and characters,
all the extremes of the human lot, and yet calls
them one body by virtue of professed allegiance
to her head.

This Christ of Humanity is even more distinct
as a personality than the Christ of Christendom,
for of that no clear conception can be formed.
We cannot imagine an individual who fills all
space, lives through all time, has a local residence
yet is everywhere, is in the literal sense a *person*,
with personal feelings, interests, thoughts and
purposes, and yet is absolutely impersonal towards
the dwellers on the earth. The idea is full of contradictions. But the Christ of Humanity is, at
least, no dream, no intellectual chimera, no theological hypothesis. He is a fact which everything
we possess and are bears witness to. History is
his autobiography; literature is his effort to utter
himself; painting and sculpture attest his feeling
of beauty; philosophy and science are the bloom-
ing of his reason; the stages of civilization are

the deep foot-tracks he has left on the surface of the planet; the great religions demonstrate the scope, quality and fervor of his soul; society, that vast, continuous, spreading organization, that mighty web of interests, institutions, codes, habits, practices, proves how real, permanent, persistent his energy has been. This Christ is at once visible and invisible; visible in actual form of living men, invisible in the shadowy recesses of antiquity, which once throbbed with life as intensely as our present does. He can be thought of as in heaven and at the same time as on earth; on earth you can see and touch him, we are part of him ourselves; in heaven, for there, in their serenity, are assembled the innumerable company who rest from their labors. The Christ of Christendom is a great assembly of powers, personified in a single man. The Christ of Humanity is a single power distributed among a multitude of men.

See how perfectly the Christ of Humanity, the Christ who is the human in Humanity, fills out the idea and discharges the function of the Christian Christ. He satifies our conception of an eternal being, for we can assign to him no beginning and we can prophecy for him no end. Time is only one of his ideas. There were ages on ages when the manifestation of him was exceedingly dim and doubtful, when he existed only in possibility, but

so he did exist, a capacity and prophecy of something undeveloped. He is omnipresent, for there
is not a spot of earth where he does not make
himself felt ; the past, the present and the future
are one in his consciousness and experience ;
through memory, activity. hope, he lives in them
all at once. He is omniscient, for he possesses
all the knowledge there is. He is omnipotent, for
he has the resources of all power. Unchangeable
he is, save with that heavenly changeableness in
which is no mutability, but only a progress from
glory to glory ; unchangeable in essence though
infinitely diversified in form. This Christ, like the
other, which is the symbol of him, is sinless ; for
the law of his perfection is in himself, and, of
course, he cannot transgress it. He is higher than
the angels, for they are but the vanished forms he
has thrown off ; he gives to the angels their angel-
hood ; the glory they shine in he creates. They
are, in fact, but the splendid reflections of his own
being from the cloudy heights of the mountain-
tops.

The Christ of Humanity has a legend as complete as that written in the New Testament. His
birth is veiled in mystery ; he seems not to have
been born as we are. Whence he came none can
tell, but in his coming kings and shepherds, angels
and oxen are alike interested. He touches all
conditions with an equal sympathy ; he is the

common property of mankind. He had his obscure, lowly period. He consecrates himself; he
has reactions of doubt and misgiving; he wrestles
with the tempter in the wilderness, is companion
of the rocks, the hot sands and the impure crawling creatures that swarm in all lonely places. He
summons the better spirits to his aid; they comfort
him. These desert passages cover whole epochs
in his experience—years, scores of years, when the
exhaustion of the moral forces seemed complete,
when the brute powers apparently had the ascend-
ency over the " son of man." He is transfigured
on the mount as he holds communion with the
celestial forms of thought that float in glory in
the upper regions of his mind. The inward voice
comforts and cheers; the heavy clouds float away
like white doves, and he comes back to his un-
congenial earth to make the powers of disease
and insanity flee away before him. He suffers
from the pain of thankless toil; he sorrows under
misunderstanding, abuse, desertion; he has his
agonies in Gethsemane when he seems to be
abandoned by all men, forsaken even by his own
diviner self, and he weeps such tears as are said
to have poured from Jesus' eyes; they drench
wide spaces and long reaches of literature with
their bitter drops; every tribe of civilized men
has books, shelves of books, saturated with this
anguish; it is the groan of human nobility in its

once so frequent hours of desolation. It is persecuted, beaten, crowned with thorns; how many times this has been done the stories of martyrdom tell, the histories of reformers staggering under their crosses, of discoverers and prophets with bleeding brows; he gives up his life; he is the great brotherhood of confessors and martyrs, among whom the choicest spirits are numbered, who sacrificed all that was dear to them rather than desert their convictions or abandon the cause of truth that was entrusted to them. This Christ verily rose from the dead, not once, but many times; for humanity cannot die, but gains new vigor from all attempts to crush it. It is glorified, exalted, to be an object of adoring contemplation, set high in heaven amid heavenly things, ranked with supreme creative powers, worshiped as what indeed it is,—the source of moral inspiration.

The narrative of the New Testament, touching but strange as the story of one individual, is sublime when read as the legend of humanity, the history of the moral nature in all individuals, the history of the human quality, the saving quality, in all mankind.

Is there any office ascribed to the Messiah of Christendom that the Christ of Humanity does not perform? Of what is to us " the world," the world of society, the civilized world, the world of interests, of politics, government, household and family concerns, art, culture, literature, religion, he is literally the creator; without him nothing of it all would exist. Of all this world of interests he is the preserver; for it is his perpetual influence that keeps them in motion. He is the incessant regenerator; for, unless unfailing supplies of human energy were furnished, the forces that gladden, cheer, improve, mature, and perfect the social world would cease to play, and a retrograde motion would at once set in.

This Christ is the Judge—and in how true, how literal a sense! Not a judge who sits aloft on a throne by the side of the Absolute God; who has open before him the record of all human actions from the beginning; who summons to his bar the spirits of the dead, confronts them with their offences, reads to them their doom, and consigns them to their retribution or their reward; not a judge who will hold a grand assize at the last day, and sentence the races of mankind according to a law he has himself established. This judge, the official judge of the popular theology, is merely a symbol of the true judge whose throne is in the moral convictions of the sensitive, educated, experienced portion of the race, whose standard is the mature moral sense of the time, whose book is the ever-open record of events, whose recording angel is the pen of the historian, the accusing memory of friend or foe, the denunciation of out-

raged sentiment, the whisper of scandal, the buzz
of gossip, the haunting testimony of conscience,
the unwritten confession of guilt, whose execu-
tioner is the public opinion of the best, the con-
demning judgment of the living heart.

Humanity, not any individual member of it, is
the final judge. The great Bar is the organized
conviction of right, so far as it has become perfected in the course of time. The best conviction
there is judges. The New Testament itself declares this. Jesus says, " He hath given him authority to execute judgment also *because he is the
son of man:*" that is, because he is human, and
the human alone can judge the human. All
beings must be judged by their peers,—angels by
angels, and men by men,—for the reason that
one's peers alone comprehend the situation, share
the experience, and can estimate the exact quality
of the offence. The judgment of men is accepted
as the judgment of God. At the bar of history
the greatest and best stand and plead, and the
verdict given is supposed to be recorded approv-
ingly in heaven. From that verdict it is difficult
to get an appeal. It often stands unchallenged
for centuries; it sometimes acquires the force of
an absolutely irreversible judgment, which the
common voice demands shall stand in the name
of moral truth, in the name of humanity. It may
be modified by the historian's research. The dis-

covery of new facts or of new interpretations may cause a revision of the sentence, and candid men may, by dint of labor, succeed in obtaining another decision, but the new verdict will be passed by the same tribunal that pronounced the first, namely, the human conscience, the enlightened moral sense of mankind, and, as before, it will be deemed ratified by the authority that sits above. In our imaginations we, like the poet Dante, consign to hell those whom we think miscreants, and give place in heaven to those whom we applaud as well-doers: and this we must do, for the voice of humanity, not necessarily the voice of the people, but the voice of the moral sentiment in the people, is regarded as the voice of God. When the scribes and pharisees howled at Jesus, and called him blasphemer because he pronounced a man's sins forgiven, he replied, " Know then that the Son of man hath power *on earth* to forgive sins." Of course he has ; that is to say, he has power to *declare* sins forgiven, to speak the word of absolution, to assure the offender that his fault is not treasured up against him.

The effort to obtain human approval of conduct is incessant, it is the only effort made. If we stand well with those who represent to us the noblest human qualities we are satisfied ; our heart is at rest ; we have no fear of the hereafter.

If but one whom we revere and love acquits us freely, on a full view of the evidence holds us blameless, we care not what the multitude of the uninstructed and passionate say; the single, intelligent, earnest, competent, judicial voice is the voice of the Christ, the voice of Humanity, the voice of God. And if that voice of friend or censor be adverse, though the air rings with the plaudits of the populace, and our own self-love resents and protests, we cannot help feeling that the face of heaven is averted from us. Humanity pardons, whether it speaks through a single voice to which our deeper nature responds, or through the voices of many. Humanity condemns, whether passing sentence in the name of public opinion, or in the name of an honored neighbor. Christ, the Judge, sits not on the clouds, he stands on the solid earth; he is not waiting for us to put off our bodily integuments and go to him; he looks us straight in the eye, and speaks into our very ears.

The Christ of Humanity is the Saviour, the physician of bodies and souls. He cures our sicknesses, expels our demons, strengthens our infirmities, works miracles of healing. He restores sight to the blind and hearing to the deaf; he makes the lame walk; he cleanses the defiled; he quickens the dying, raises the dead; he opens the prison-house, gives liberty to the captives, lightens the burdens that press on the poor and miserable. Since the beginning of time he has toiled terribly to teach the ignorant, recall the erring, reclaim the wicked, stir the dull mind, soften the hard heart, awaken to life the dormant soul. He has taught in cities, towns, villages, on hillsides, from fishing-boats, beneath marble porticoes and temple roofs, under the blue canopy of the sky, reasoning with philosophers, remonstrating with bigots, preaching to simple men and women. He has set a steadfast example of temperance, chastity, truth, pity. He has gone into the wilderness in search of stray sheep; he has pursued the moral leper into his desolated haunts among the graves; he has spent himself, worn himself out, literally died in poverty and outward wretchedness in order that the mission of brotherly love might be accomplished through him. He is the glorious company of the philosophers; he is the noble army of reformers and philanthropists; he is the holy band of the wise in heart who counsel warn, admonish and console the world.

There have been Christians who held that their Christ was very God, the sole and absolute Deity, that beside and beyond him was no other godhead, the godhead being all taken up and exhausted in him; they compressed the whole trinity into his person. The Church declared this view to be heresy, and condemned it. There are those, Auguste Comte at the head of them, who hold that their Christ of humanity is very God, all the God there is, that the Grand Man exhausts the conception of absolute Being. But this view is thus far pronounced heresy by the leaders of philosophic thought. The Christ of Christendom is not regarded as being the Eternal Father; he may be co-eternal with him, co-equal with him, a full and clear reflection of him, an express image of him, but he is not identical with him. The godhead would not be complete without him, and yet he is not the godhead. The moon's reflection on the surface of the lake is not the moon.

Humanity, taken in its most comprehensive sense, is but a reflection after all of deity. We can, without a severe strain of mind, imagine its total destruction. It lives, so far as we know, on a single planet, one of the least glorious of the solar system. It is not inconceivable that, in the course of countless ages, the planet, with all that inhabit and inherit it, may be blotted out of space. Would the destruction of the human species involve the destruction of the first cause of the universe? Would the career of the world be brought to a sudden termination and the order of things be at once dissolved? The human race is still at the mercy of the cosmic forces; a considerable change in temperature, malaria in the atmosphere, failure of crops, pestilence, sweeps mankind off by tens of thousands. Do these frightful catastrophes jeopardize in the smallest degree the interest of the vast creation, do they weaken the creative elements or drain of their vital power the laws of evolution under whose superintendence and beneath whose active control the all of things goes on perfecting itself through the millions of generations? It is fair to regard Humanity as the incarnate deity of mankind; but the decease of mankind would not cause faintness in the perfect being whose lineaments mankind may reflect, whose laws mankind may organize and illustrate, but whose possibility mankind can scarcely be supposed to exhaust.

Between the Unsearchable One and imperfect beings, the Christ of Humanity perpetually mediates, passing down to the low places the light of regenerating influence, leading up the weak and timid souls to the mountain-top whence they may behold diviner forms and hear more celestial voices than come to them in their ordinary lives. He touches both extremes; his earthly lot associates him with lowliness and poverty, his character allies him with translated and immortal spirits. The true Christ reaches all heights and sounds all deeps. He eats with sinners and communes with Moses and Elias. There is a stain on his mortal birth, yet he dwells in heaven.

That humanity needs a Christ will not here be argued; we may take its own word for that. It professes ever to have one, though he be but the attenuated shadow of a theological dogma. It shudders at the thought of being left without one, and lashes itself into spasms of rage against those whom it suspects of a design to take its Christ or even its figment, its dim, vaporous dream or fancy of a Christ, away. The denial of the Christ is held to be the last impiety ; it seems to be a denial of all that is wise and true in the world. People cannot exaggerate the bereavement they should be in without him. They who fancy that this feeling is in great measure affected are probably deceived : it has all the appearance of being genuine and profound. They who think it is the artificial product of theological education are perhaps mistaken. The theology may quite possibly have been a product of the feeling ; the need of the Christ may have called into being the philosophy of the Christ.

But if this were so, the need must have been for a real Christ, a true incarnation in flesh and blood living among men, and this Christ could have been no other than the greatest souls among themselves, the best they knew, whether that best were near them or far off. These they transfigured and translated ; their name they conjured by ; in their name they worshipped. The Christ was precious for what he represented, rather than for what he was. He glorified common qualities ; he set the seal on principles that all share ; he made illustrious the spirit of goodness that has its lowly, retired shrine in every heart ; he placed the candle of the individual conscience by the side of the sun, and set each sparkle of humanity in the firmament as a star. He is the symbol of that essential human nature which is the Messiah cradled in the bosom of every man.

V.

ATONEMENT.

THE ministry of religion, whether evangelical or otherwise, is a ministry of reconciliation, —reconciliation between whom or what? What are the two things that stand over against one another, and between which it would make peace? The older, and still the prevalent, mode of thinking puts the antagonism thus: Separation between man and God; opposition of nature to the supernatural; conflict of the material with the spiritual; a gulf dividing this world from the next; the two dooms,—salvation and damnation, hell and heaven. The chasm was one that divided the finite from the Infinite, and it cut its way sheer from the primal origin and essence of being, down through every department of thought and life; parting off into two definite portions the spiritual, moral, social, personal interests of mankind; cleaving in twain cares and pleasures, mercantile pursuits and trivial amusements; setting man at variance with himself along the whole line of his existence; making his experience a warfare; opening a cross-road at every step of his temporal career, and at the end of it showing a parting of the ways in the direction of everlasting life or everlasting death. Thus, from man's origin to his endlessness, the imagination disclosed a succession of gulfs which only wings of the spirit could traverse. It has been the business of late years to fill up these gulfs. The gulf between God and man is filled by conceiving man as, on one side of his nature, *divine :* and God as, on one side of his nature, *human.* There is a province, it is said, where God and man meet, without the aid of intercession. He is not far from every one of us, and may be found by all that seek him. We in our better hours recline upon his bosom and inhale his peace. If we do not meet him in the workshop or the street, the fault is ours. If we do not live in companionship with him, it is not because we cannot, but because we will not. There is no chasm: there need, therefore, be no bridge.

The gulf between nature and the supernatural is filled by extending the realm of the natural till it includes all the phenomena that come under our intellectual cognizance. The natural we say, is the orderly, the regular, the beautiful, the perfect. The natural man is the good man. The natural and the spiritual man are one. Is it said the " natural " is that which is under law? Every thing is under law. There are laws of thought

and feeling : the Supreme Holiness is bound : the
First Cause is necessary. To be released from
law is to be outcast, not free. The gulf between
matter and spirit is filled by making matter the
organ of spirit; spirit the impelling force, matter
the means of manifestation ; spirit the intelligent
cause, matter the pliant instrument; spirit the
active principle, matter the passive substance,—
the two necessary to balance, complete, and use
each other. Spirit without matter, an unorganized, diffusive power ; matter without spirit a non-
entity. Instead of a gulf betwixt the two needing
to be escaped, a connection between the two so
close as to be indissoluble.

The gulf between this world and the next is
filled by throwing both into one; by making life
one continuous whole ; by abolishing the grave as
a receptacle of consciousness, or a goal of proba-
tion, or a check to advance, and running all the
lines of moral experience straight through it;
grading the pit into which the body plunges, and
setting on either side of the dark valley the watch
lights of hope, that sparkle on, far as the eye can
see, lighting the one unmistakable road that leads
to universal blessedness all the souls of men.

In similar wise disappears the gulf between
finite and infinite. The finite, we say, has its infinite possibilities. The human is not shut in by
a wall. Its horizon line recedes as its being ex-

pands. This *mortal* puts on immortality, this *corruptible* puts on incorruption. The infinite is the moral, the spiritual, the perfect. But the finite tends to these, and, following its tendency, reaches them.

In these few words, so few as to be unintelligible possibly, we try to indicate the work attempted by the intellectual energies of our generation,—the work undertaken by science and philosophy, by ethics, politics, art; in a word, by intelligence using all the means that thought and experience place at its command to abolish the separation between things human and things divine.

The apparent result is the cessation of a ministry of reconciliation. There is nothing, apparently, to reconcile. The atonement is not *to be* made; it was made from the beginning. The atonement is laid in the nature of things. The cry therefore is, that the prophet shall give up his ghost of a mission; that the preacher shall abandon his mere tradition of a calling, shall put an end to his pantomime of gesticulation, and earn his living as other men earn theirs. For the pulpit, we are told, there is no place: take it away. A gentleman had running through his grounds the Middlesex Canal. It divided his garden from a very beautiful grove of trees, which was a favorite retreat in the summer

time. Being a man of wealth, he spanned the
canal with a stone bridge elegant to behold. After
a time the railroad superseded the canal. The
waters were drawn off. The bed was filled in,
planked over, covered with corn-fields; but the
bridge still stands where it did. It serves no purpose as a bridge; it is easier to walk over the
even ground than it is to climb its steep arch; it
occupies good soil for planting; it withdraws
from use a quantity of granite; it is by no means
ornamental; and its incongruity raises a smile,
not always inaudible, in the passers-by. So, to
the apprehension of many, stands the pulpit, now
that the dividing gulf is dry,—a needless relic of a
past dispensation, doing nothing that literature,
the book, the magazine, the newspaper, do not
accomplish a great deal better; and, by its stand-
ing.where it does, casting a tacit reproach, and
being an actual hindrance to these.

Let us consider if this is a fair statement of the
whole case. Is the ministry of reconciliation
ended? Are the gulfs all filled up? Let us admit that certain maps of them have been rendered
useless; that the charts of the old engineers have
become obsolete; that ancient estimates of their
character, dimensions, and depth have been dis-
credited; that their names have become unintelligible. But has the ancient ravine itself been
abolished? If it has been, the ministry of recon-

ciliation has been abolished; if it has not been, that ministry remains, and it becomes us to consider the way in which it shall be discharged.

To my apprehension, the gulf, the essential gulf, the only gulf that is worth practically considering, is the gulf *betwixt the animal and the human elements in man.* You may describe it under the old nomenclature, if you will. Call it a gulf between the creature and the Creator, between the temporal and the eternal, between the finite and the infinite, between the worldly and the heavenly life, between the flesh and the spirit, you will not convey a stronger impression of its reality or its character than you do when you call it a gulf between the animal and the human in his constitution.

The real facts of life are unaltered by time. There has been no change in the substance of things. The structure of the mind and the material of experience remain as they were. The *interpretations* of life vary. The *realities* of life are immutable. The data to which the older divines appealed in justification of their ministry, are still before us. Human existence is full of them; human nature teems with them; and an earnest glance discloses them to us in a form as solemn and startling as that which moved once to cries and tears.

It is enough to hint at these things, I cannot

describe them. Ignorance, weakness, imbecility, lethargy, stupor, vice, stubbornness, turpitude, lie in monstrous heaps upon our civilization; and the wind of passion, which is always blowing in gusts, now and then catches them, whirls them in the air, stifles us with their dust, and covers us with their rubbish. Terrible surprises lurk in the moral atmosphere. A little congealed vapor in winter is driven before the soft air; while we sleep, the light particles of snow fall by myriads. A muffled army of invasion, they take possession of the earth; we wake in the morning to find ourselves blockaded,—the streets impassable, lines of railroad buried beneath avalanches; mechanical power, steam power, is set at defiance; the irresistible legions of the travelling public are held under arrest: the lord of the planet battles for existence with snow-flakes.

So in the moral world about us are stored the elements of terror. Of a sudden they gather, they drive upon us; the virtue of man buffets them in vain. The *obstinacy* of the dark power is what appalls us. This animal element, this crude element of passionateness,—by whatever name you will call it,—this dumb, chaotic, portentous force, sweeps over us, and bears down feeling, purpose, determination. Better than volumes of divinity, the daily papers present the argument for a kind of inertness in the moral world.

The story of the warfare between the powers of
light and the powers of darkness is as new as it is
old. Every earnest man and woman is conscious
of it. Paul's terrible language—"That which I
do, I disavow; what I would, I do not; what I
hate, I do"—is hardly too strong to describe the
pressure of inability that is upon individuals and
society. A vast burden of powerlessness weighs
will and purpose down; a rigid limitation sets
bounds to our effort. We see so much farther
than we reach, we perceive so much more than
we can do, we confess so many obligations we
cannot meet, we are aware of so many duties
we cannot discharge! Our purpose faints behind
our desire; our thought gropes after our dream;
our determinations are determined. We know
that things are wrong; but we cannot get a conviction that they are wrong, and so we go on
doing them with a fatal facility that makes us feel
ourselves creatures of destiny. Blundering and
impotent, we push on, hoping that somehow
things will come out right, but haunted by a desperate feeling, that, if they do, it will be in spite
of ourselves.

Now these, I apprehend, are the old facts out
of which the old theory of a dislocated world was
constructed. This passion, this prejudice, this
inertness, this perversity, this incapacity, this old
man of the sea, sitting astride of our shoulders,

suggested the thing that was called the " Old
Adam " in us.   What is it if it is not the *old
Adam,*—precisely that and nothing else?   It is
the immaturity of mankind ; it is the crudeness of
human nature ; it is the heavy bulk of the raw
material which we have not organized ; it · is the
mud of the pre-Adamite world clinging to our
feet ; the preceding centuries huddle their infirmities on our backs ; their ideas infest our minds ;
their practices entangle our footsteps ; their judgments nestle in the meshes of our law ; their lusts,
violences, dishonesties, mingle with our feelings.
Their influence is akin to that of demoniacal possession.   To it we may trace all, or nearly all, the
social enormities that curse us.   A great many
things we do that are lawless, or worse ; yet it is
not *we* that do them, but this force of unsubdued
animalism that is in us.   Is it to be wondered at,
that, in ages of ignorance, when human reason
was unable to take scientific views of things, men
cried out for an Expiator to lift off an incubus
that was too dreadful to be carried?

But to call for an Expiator would be vain.   No
expiation will serve.   It is inheritance we suffer
from, not guilt ; undevelopment, not depravity ;
infirmity, not sin.   The struggle is between history and possibility ; the *want* of humanity and
the *promise* of humanity ; the *beastliness* we have
not outgrown, and the *saintliness* we have not ap-

propriated. And we are to end the conflict, not by throwing ourselves in agony upon the merits of a Redeemer, but by throwing ourselves enthusiastically upon the virtue of our rational powers.

It is here that the ministry of reconciliation comes in. Its office is to pass men over the gulf that *yawns between the lower and the higher self;* to rescue humanity from passion to principle; to redeem it from selfishness into self-love; to counteract the brutal traditions of sensuality and hate by the beautiful prophecies of sacrifice and brotherhood. The preacher represents the *human nature* in men as the supreme element in them, and for the interests of that human nature he stands, as a distinct interest, never to be compromised. The difference between the developed and the undeveloped man, the cultured and the uncultured, the human and the bestial, while in one sense it is a difference of more or less, is in another sense a contrast of opposites. There are no gulfs betwixt men, we say, only differences of level. But a difference of level makes Niagara. At the top of the precipice, laughing lovers sit on the grass, admiring the rainbow; at the bottom boils the caldron of death; and between top and bottom there is no inch of space where existence is possible for a moment.

A difference of more or less! You take ship in New York, and sail out on the Atlantic. You pursue a level course. There is no dip or plunge, save as the waves lift or depress the vessel's prow. On and on you go ; overhead the constellations, around the monotonous plain of waters : night and day, for weeks and weeks, you go on. At length you come to port on the *other side of the globe.* It seems to you that, were your vision long enough, you might look back and see the city you started from. Not unless you can look *round* the planet or *through* it. Between you and home is the solid globe. It was only a question of miles, more or fewer ; but here you are setting the soles of your feet against those of your friends in Broadway, and pointing your heads in opposite directions. More or less makes the antipodes.

Look at the ideas that lie in groups on the surface of the religious world. Mark their distribution among the different sects. There seems to be no line of radical separation between them. They are shared by the various churches. Some have more of this, others more of that,—more or less of depravity ; more or less of the Christ ; more or less of inspiration ; more or less of grace through usage or rite ; more or less of authority conceded to book or confession ; more or less of duration to punishment, or of destination to bliss. The question is one of shading. So it appears ; *but it is not as it appears.* When Luther put off from Rome, he had no thought of going far. His successors looked but a little way beyond Luther. Their successors pushed on the line of advance, nothing being further from their purpose than a final departure from the ancient landmarks. So sect followed sect, each modifying slightly one or more of the original beliefs, but each persuaded it was keeping every essential article; each, in fact, convinced that it brought the essential article out into the light. So church follows church, and party party; all holding fast by the same tradition, all taking their bearings from the same star, all consulting the same charts, all studying the same authorities in navigation, all sailing under the same flag, heading for the same port, carrying the same freight of souls. Universalism came, Unitarianism, Liberalism,—all using the same forms, all observing the same sacraments, all reading the same Bible, all making the same ascriptions in prayer and hymn. There were successive *departures*, but no visible *gulf.* There were innumerable shades of opinion; but no sharp line of division was evident, cutting Christendom in two. But look beneath the surface, and there it is! As they sailed round the globe, these timid navigators found the *antipodes*, and now stand greeting each other with the soles of their feet, their eyes straining at opposite quarters of the heavens. For while the old church stood on the dogma of human *depravity*, the new church stands on faith in human *ability*. The old church planted itself on the idea that men must be miraculously saved from hell; the new church plants itself on the idea that men must distance hell by reason. The old church bowed the soul to an institution; the new church makes institutions the creatures of the soul. And between these two groups of principles a gulf is fixed, so deep and wide that they who stand on one side cannot see those who stand on the other.

In society people look much alike : save in some little peculiarities of feature, walk, mien, manner, mood, there is not much apparent difference. They profess about the same average opinions, applaud about the same class of sentiments, approve about the same courses of conduct. Human nature, we hear people say, is about the same all over the world. The differences between men are simply differences of more or less. And yet it needs no keen observer to note certain very plain distinctions as between people who live as if the *world were made for them*, and people who live *as if they were made for the world*. One principle bids a man to live *for himself*; another principle bids a man live *for others*. The principles stand to each other as light and darkness,—in ceaseless opposition. They writhe together, day and night, in every soul.

We hear and see a great deal of the extremes

in human condition and character. They are indeed astonishing, overwhelming in their extent. Humanity has its head in the heavens and its feet in the mire. Its soul dwells with the angels, its senses grovel with the beasts; it prays on the mountain-tops, and wallows in the pit. In its heart are the eight paradises and the corresponding hells. Imagination will hardly scale the serene heights where it communes with the Eternal, imagination will hardly pierce the gloomy abysses where it mingles with unclean things.

The gulf that all see is the gulf that yawns between the extremes of human condition, between the rich who lay the world under contribution to gratify their desire, and the poor who cannot command a crust to support their life; between the well who feel existence to be a boon, and the sick to whom it is an agony; between the happy whose being is flooded with daily sunshine, and the wretched who dread the breaking of the dawn; between the high in station who look down on whole orders of their fellow-creatures, and the obscure whom even the insignificant and the unprivileged look down upon. The contemplation of these vast differences sickens the heart and depresses faith; the suffering that springs from them saddens the earth; the bitterness and hate and strife they engender make acrid the thoughts of the reflecting and the feelings of the good.

And yet the distance between these extremes in human condition seems to vanish away when we consider the distance between the extremes of human character. Think of the man who is perfectly self-contained, even, calm, steadfast, whose desires are all subordinated to reason, whose passions always serve, whose clear intelligence never loses sight of supreme truths, whose will never swerves from lofty principles, whose faith is never dim, whose hope is never clouded, whose joy is never disturbed by fear or disappointment, whose moral powers work with the precision and smoothness of a perfect mechanism, and then think of the man who is not self-centred at all, who is not self-respecting, who is barely self-conscious, who is the sport of his desires, the victim of his passions, who never uses reason, knows not what principle may be, never casts a thought above, never throws a prudent anticipation forward, never gazes seriously within, but drifts and rolls and tumbles and is beaten up and down by every chance wave that strikes him. Think of the man who lives in and for others, who is continually giving himself out with a generosity that has no limits, a kindness that is never chilled, a disinterestedness that has no after-thought ; a philanthropist such as we can all think of; and then think of the man who lives in and for himself, with a grossness of appetite, a greediness for

gain, an insatiableness of ambition that holds no
right sacred, no person inviolable, no condition
respectable; a man who plunders and steals, and
gorges himself, utterly heedless of the misery he
creates, the ruin he causes, the wrong he commits,
the grief, the despair, the brutality he occasions.
Think of the difference between a Borromeo and
a Borgia, between a John Howard and a James
Fisk! It is the difference between heaven and
earth; it is the difference between heaven and
hell.

And yet this gulf, this deep, bottomless, moral
abyss, is generally concealed from view. Being
internal, it is unperceived. They who dwell on
either brink may be unaware of its existence.
They who dwell on the lower edge of it are very
seldom conscious of it. Self-satisfied, complacent,
lapped in their vanity, absorbed by their sensations, they may be, and often are, wholly ignorant
of the moral condition of others, and wholly un-
suspicious of any superiority on the part of saint
or philanthropist. A gulf exists, not filled up, not
bridged over, not seen across. Not only is there
no atonement,—no at-one-ment,—no reconciliation, no intercourse, no accord, there is no sus-
picion that such a thing is needful, possible, or
desirable.

It may happen, however, that one of these people on the lower edge of the chasm may catch a

glimpse of a shining form on the other side. He takes up the biography of a noble person; he hears a tale of heroism; he meets a kindling character; he is touched, thrilled by a searching word or a splendid deed, and strange emotions seize him. Like a beggar suddenly thrust into a company of ladies and gentlemen, he feels his clothes, sees his nakedness and is ashamed; a sense of meanness and foulness and squalor comes to him for the first time; his rank corruption is offensive to his own soul; he loathes, despises, hates himself; covers his face with his hands, and tries to slink off. A desire is born in him to make himself more decent outside and inside, that he may be fit for the company of this exalted person. He exaggerates possibly both his own unworthiness and the other's worth. The apparition seems that of an angel, a demi-god, and he sinks to the earth, like a base, sinful creature who needs complete renewing before being qualified even for the glorious one's pity.

Something like this was experienced by the people on whom the vision of Jesus broke. The manifestation of a soul so spotless white, so saintly and at the same time so sweet, so pure yet so pitiful, so true and so tender, so lofty and withal so lowly, so free from all taint of sensuality and so compassionate towards the sensual, so heavenly-minded yet so earnest, so contemplative yet so practical, so spiritual and all the while so human, troubled, yes, convulsed the thoughtless, easy, self-satisfied minds of those who came across it. The demons of the tomb cried out when he came near; guilty passion poured forth its avowal in his presence; turpitude bewailed its blackness and wept itself faint at his feet; fires of aspiration began to burn; bitter drops of penitence began to fall. A sudden consciousness of infirmity deepening into sin was begotten, and started the great wave of experience that rolled over the first two centuries and left its traces on every continent of the human mind.

Paul was one of the first to interpret this experience and to show a way by which the terrible sense of sin might be appeased. Pointing to the sinless Christ, dwelling on his loneliness and condescension, appealing to his voluntarily assumed suffering and sorrow, insisting above all on his humanity, which all, even the poorest, the lowest, the guiltiest shared with him, he cried: Believe in him, have faith in the reality of this goodness, have faith in your possible participation in it, and the gulf between you will shrink till it disappears: you will be invigorated; your old nature will be taken away, a new nature will be bestowed; fear will give place to hope, sorrow to joy, hatred to charity. The ancient woe of the world, alienation, bitterness and death will cease, the broken unity of the race will be restored.

I have been describing the genesis of the doctrine of the Atonement, the reconciliation of the sensual man with the spiritual, the atonement of the animal in human nature with the angel.

The Christian theology dramatized this existence, put it into mythological form. Jesus represents the supreme purity of the Eternal. Over against him in violent contrast, in black opposition in fact, stands the human race, corrupt, depraved, helpless, unable to make a motion towards its own felicity, abandoned to misery, doomed to perdition. Jesus, the Christ, the Lord of heaven, the ideal man, the pure spirit of humanity, leaves his serene heights, descends from his pinnacle of glory, grapples this disconsolate humanity by the heart-strings, touches it, melts it with his sympapathy, wins it, invites it, persuades it, softens it, breaks its heart, compels it to confess kindred with him, drags out the possibilities of good that had lain dormant till they had well nigh perished, restores ideally, and leaves them to restore actually, the union that was indispensable to their life, and returns to the place whence he came to pour down a steady influence which shall in time draw the extremes of humanity together, and effect a perfect society where before no society had existed.

The allegory is as beautiful as it is bold, but it is an allegory. Taken literally as describing a condition of things, as recording a historical fact or a series of facts, it is as wild as the legendary tales of the nativity. But taken practically, it covers and symbolizes truths that cannot safely be neglected. As a dogma or a group of dogmas it falls to pieces at a touch; the attempt to explain it demolishes it; none have so effectually expressed its contradictions as its friends; but as a piece of imagination it pictures things of deep experience. Let us try to ascertain what these are.

Mankind present hideous extremes of condition and character, and yet in mankind no interval breaks the unity; no abyss sunders the cord or swallows the identity. Sage and simpleton, saint and sinner, are of kin. The ideal man touches both extremes of condition, is at home among all experiences, sympathizes with all character. In the Christ all are taught that they are ideally, and may be actually, one. There is a fellow-feeling, unrecognized perhaps, but deep and instinctive, that grapples the elements of the race together with living bonds. Inasmuch as the extremes affect each other, they meet. England's pauperism tells on England's queen. The squalor of Rome loads the atmosphere which the vicar of Christ inhales. The richest man on the Fifth Avenue is in daily peril from the festering, rotting, poisoning poverty that breeds contagion in his

tenement-houses, and nurses the demon of fever
in damp cellars and noisome yards. There is not
a philosopher whose mind does not suffer in its
texture and delicacy from the mass of ignorance
that sinks whole continents of intelligence beneath
its foul waters. The saint's prayer struggles
through the vapors that infest the moral atmosphere, and make it too thick for blithesome aspiration. The reformer's ardor is weighed down by
the inertia of undeveloped conscience, and the
love of the philanthropist sighs and gasps from
the inhumanity he is never himself in contact
with, yet never can escape from. New York
shudders at the mention of cholera working on
the Bosphorus, and the tidings of convulsions on
the Pacific coast make its state insecure.

Humanity has but one life, breathes but one
atmosphere, draws sustenance from one central
orb. To be reconciled with humanity, to feel the
common pulse, is life; to be alienated from humanity, to have no share in the common vitality,
is death. The slightest material separation is felt
disastrously.

Let one withdraw but a short distance from
the centre of humane civilizing influence, let one
go but a few miles out of the reach of easy intercourse, unless he be possessed of uncommon mental resources, or of a genuine love of nature and
the pursuits of country life, he suffers from the

want of incessant contact with his kind or class ;
he has attacks of *ennui*, becomes restless or dull.
Let him go further still, out of the reach of newspapers, books, and sympathetic fellowship through
the church or society, and the effect is still more
disastrous; the mind slumbers, feeling becomes
slow and heavy, interest slackens and narrows,
the range of ideas contracts, the higher operations
of intelligence cease, a species of animalism
begins to affect the spirit; there is an unmistakable tendency backward and downward. Let him
retire to a still greater distance ; let him go quite
out of reach of his kind, where he cannot command the ordinary supplies of life, and it is with
the utmost difficulty that he continues in existence ; he must dispense with clothing, have no
cover for limbs, feet or head, subsist on such
herbs, berries, and roots as the ground produces
spontaneously ; for he has no tools of labor, no
gun, no fish-hook, no snare, no weapons; he cannot plunder the wild beast of his skin, and, unless nature provides him with a hairy coat, he perishes. Your Swiss Family Robinson is a self-help-
ing community, with all the resources of humanity
stored up in a miraculous bag. Your Robinson
Crusoe has with him the fine results of civilization, is himself a community of trained abilities,
and calls humanity to his side in the shape of a
Man Friday; the ship in which he was wrecked

was a magazine of human powers which came to
his rescue and support; he is only apparently
and temporarily alone; the vital cord of industry,
temperance, skill, trained intelligence, strong
moral purpose, holds him to his allegiance, spans
the gulf that separates him from his far-off kindred, and like the oceanic cable transmits to him
the pulsation of the powerful, full-blooded humanity to which he belongs.

Should a man, like one I knew, refuse to share
the common burden of expense by deliberately
and stubbornly declining to pay his taxes, he
being abundantly able to do it, the consequences
would be immediately felt in the cessation of those
offices of assistance and maintenance that are indispensable to the life of a community. He would
be a self-banished outlaw, having no claim on the
protection which society guarantees to its members, no right to call on the policeman, no title to
appeal to the courts, no power to enforce his law-
ful dues from others, no pledge to give to others
that will make them willing to trust him. The
tradesman may decline to deal with him, having
no legal security against his dishonesty; the laborer may refuse to work for him, except for
money paid down in advance; he might be robbed
and the community would not care; though he
were annoyed and maltreated and abused, he
would have no redress: he has broken one of the

ties, one of the conventional ties, it may be, that link him with the common lot, and the process of active decomposition takes place.

Benedict Arnold betrayed a national trust, and instantly was deceased as an American. It was in vain that he spoke of the affection he still held for his country ; his country held none for him. It was idle for him to write to General Washington of " a heart conscious of its own rectitude : " his flight to the enemy proved that he knew such an assertion would be met with derision. The very enemy to which he deserted did not believe him, but made him know by repeated insults, by continual manifestations of disgust and horror, and by abandonment to utter obscurity, that he had forfeited the respect of his fellow men. He was cast forth as a branch, and withered.

An animal individualism sets up its title to do not what it ought, but what it chooses; to enact, not its duty but its whim. It will make as many drunkards as it pleases ; it will ruin as many as it finds agreable to ruin at the gambling table ; it will convulse the finances of the country by selfish and fraudulent tricks in speculation ; it will flout the marriage-bond, and have a fresh husband or a fresh wife once a week if it be so inclined ; it will parade all manner of indecencies of thought and conduct before the public gaze, and will coolly justify them on the ground that it is nobody's business but its own. But it is everybody's business, and that it is everybody's business becomes at once apparent from the stern sentence of moral excommunication which is pronounced, and no sooner pronounced than carried into effect; society disowns those who thus insolently set up for themselves. There is a noble individualism that discards conventional usage of fashion, that will not conform to the superficial habits of the world, but all the more acknowledges allegiance to the laws of justice, truth, honor, reason, to the higher humanity; this kind of individualism confesses its dependence and the need of keeping that dependence close and radical; its roots are struck deep down in the primitive soil, and bring thence perpetual supplies of vigor; it is like a forest tree that indeed stands alone, but which through its multitudinous fibres searches the ground for food, and keeps itself in most vital sympathy with the all-quickening planet. Such individualism is most cordially human. But the animal individualism I speak of, which is simply a base hunger for pleasurable sensations, bears its professors down to lower and lower strata of society, and leaves them at last among the swine, gladly filling their bellies with the husks that swine do eat. They become by-words of scandal, synonyms of reproach. They are sundered from all saving and fructifying intercourse ; their upper faculties decay one by one ; the power to appreciate fine examples is lost ; they are sloughed off like a useless shred of skin.

Even the failure actively to serve humanity by some kind of industry, kindness, helpfulness, human pitifulness and good will, is visited by the same condemnation. Indolence weakens the vital bond of mutual service, and entails a corresponding feebleness of impulse, faintness of will, and dreaminess of purpose. Faculty ebbs away, self-respect declines, and existence trickles along in very shallow channels. Vice more fatally kills the root of moral power than it saps the physical force. The drunkard's body may outlast the century, but it will be half that time a tomb. The frame of the debauchee may brave the wear and tear of dissipation for threescore years and ten, but long before that his soul will have ceased to molest it. The dust may hold together, but the spirit will have fled. Humanity has no interest in the man, and there is for him no help.

Salvation is in the Christ, says the Church. Salvation is in the human Christ, the Christ of humanity, say we. It is a salvation by Faith and also by Works ; faith incorporating the individual with society through sympathy with the principles by virtue of which society exists, and works making that incorporation compact and solid through some positive contribution of service rendered to one or more human beings, service according to ability as respects kind and degree, service of hand, thought, feeling or purpose ; service done publicly or privately, openly or secretly, matters not, service perpetual or incidental, continuous or intermittent, as occasion determines ; it is all good and saving, so it be done sincerely, done in kindness, done in the spirit of humanity. A cup of cold water *in the name of a disciple*, that is, given in pure human kindness, will not lose its reward. " He who has done it unto the least of these has done it unto me." It is not the deed, it is not the object : it is the *spirit* that identifies the greatest and the least. The humblest part of the body belongs to the noblest part by virtue of an *organic connection.*

The spirit of humanity is all. We must once more lay stress on that. The Christ is human. He is not a Pharisee, a Sadducee, a priest : he is a man. Incorporation with a branch of humanity will not suffice ; the individual must stand well, not with his order, class, guild, clique, with any fragment of the human heart and conscience, but with the whole. The general heart absolves ; the common conscience justifies. The caste spirit, under the most attenuated form, is detrimental to moral health. This man lives in his family, lives there loyally and affectionately, but lives there only. He loves his wife because she is his wife; his children because they belong to him; his home because it is the private retreat of his idle, self-indulgent hours. To all outside he is indifferent and cold; the interests of the community at large are nothing to him; the moral condition of the society about him gives him no concern; he rejects politics, he hates the word "reform," he disengages himself from the bonds of sympathy which his fellow-beings impose on each other, and lives in entire devotion, and in all but entire isolation. Even his interest in his family is not human. The humanity of his wife and children, their moral culture, the state of their interior dispositions, the quality of their affections, does not concern him. Another man lives in his profession and the technicalities of it. However devoted he may be to its interests,—and the more devoted he is to its interests as a *profession*, the more he loses of his humanity,—the professional garb, manner, mode of speech, separate him from his kind; professional pride, envy, jealousy, affect his mind injuriously. The lawyer who is only an attorney, the physician who is merely a doctor, the minister who forgets in his cloth the wide sympathy that is more than all churches and creeds and holy men, is so far defunct. Wealth furnishes untold, inestimable advantages to its possessor ; the wealthy class is an indispensable part of the community. An ingenious critic contended that the Christ could not have been so very poor, because a gentleman invited him to dinner, and he wore a seamless coat which none but the wealthy could afford. To belong to the wealthy class is a privilege ; but he who prides himself on belonging to this class, who holds its class interests peculiarly sacred, protects them against the encroachments of the moral sentiment, bribes legislators to support them, takes pains to hold aloof from people who are not rich, flaunts his opulence in the face of the world, and cares not who suffers, so long as he and his flourish, —this man is many degrees removed from his kind ; he has much to do before he can be considered reconciled with those he plunders and outrages.

It was said lately again, that before there can be refinement of spirit, grace of bearing, gentleness and suavity of disposition, there must be an aristocracy ; that aristocracies alone have produced ladies and gentlemen. This is what the Southern people said of themselves, and what their Northern parasites said of them, before the war. Much was told of their elegance, their delicacy of sentiment, their fine instinct of propriety, their social dignity and breeding. Yes : these qualities were all there, but, being qualities peculiar to a caste, they were essentially inhuman. Those Southern people, along with these qualities, and *as the reverse side of them,* had and openly exhibited dispositions of coldness, pride, contempt, cruelty, that were even shocking to contemplate ; they boasted of qualities that cut them off from their kind; they plumed themselves on their indolence, their luxuriousness, their superiority to the vulgar herd of workers and tradesmen ; they cherished disorganizing feelings ; they fomented destructive passions ; their theory of society was that of barbarians; for honesty they read honor, and the symbol of honor among them was the pistol. They were the most ornamental people in America, certainly, the most sleek and glossy and insinuating ; but the backwoodsman in Maine was a better specimen of human nature.

The largest section of humanity does not contain the human. A nationality is not big enough. The patriot who is nothing but a patriot, a German, Frenchman, Englishman, American, is less than the simplest man who respects his fellow-being without further qualification. The good Samaritan of the parable, with but two pence in his pocket, was nearer the Christ's heart than the whole band of stormy patriots who had their banners all ready to unfurl in the cause of the soldier king. The passion of patriotism keeps occasions of discord open ; it multiplies them, and exults in the aggrandizement of its own state at the expense of its neighbors; it counts the profits it may derive from foreign disaster and foreign war. It is essentially *inhuman*.

The problem of atonement is to reconcile the opposite extremes of humanity by creating in all men faith in the human elements that are in them all. The atonement is not completed when the Christ has done his part. It is then only made possible; its conditions are given, nothing more. The reconciliation is effected when men do their part. But to make them do their part is the difficult point, to beget in them faith and love. According to theologians the sacrifice of Christ met the preliminaries, nothing more. It made the atonement possible. If he had done the whole the old Antinomian Universalism would be justified which claimed that all were of necessity saved, because Christ died for all. The sufferings of the divine man are the ground of reconciliation, but the ground must be occupied. The higher powers have done their best: it remains for the lower powers to respond. So far as heaven is concerned the atonement is complete; ideally, the reconciliation is effected; practically, a very large part of the work is yet to be done.

Christian divines are still laboring at the task of impressing upon mankind in general the necessity of being spiritually incorporated with their

Christ, of taking the hand he extends to them and rushing into the arms he spreads open to take them in. They dilate with enthusiasm on his goodness, his condescension in leaving his heavenly seats to help them, his kindness to mortal distress, his patience with infirmity, dullness, and guilt, his pity for suffering, his compassion with sorrow, his graciousness in accepting the most humiliating earthly conditions, his magnanimity in defending the weak cause, his devotion in dying, his sacrifice in giving up his very life for a race which only the utmost charity could induce him to regard with even so much as mercy. The story of his superhuman, his altogether heavenly loveliness, is told over and over again, with endless exaggeration and touching eloquence, is pressed home with all the force of cumulative appeal, in the hope that insensible, callous, stupid, vicious, abandoned men and women will at length be reached and penetrated, convinced and subdued by it, that the heart of sin will be broken, and the sick-souled, penitent prodigal be brought home. Faith in the effect of this presentation has been unqualified. Take it where you will, the church said, do it justice, press it home upon the harlot, the murderer, the blasphemer, the atheist, and it will do the work of regeneration. The story has been told so often that everybody has heard it, and never will it be told more pleadingly. The effects have in a measure followed. They still follow. Conversions have been made—are made yet—where the heart is quite simple, and the way to it unimpeded. But the atonement is far enough yet from being accomplished. The Christ of the church is fading into remoter distance day by day, his figure is becoming smaller and smaller in proportion to the modern world, his voice is less distinctly heard amid the din of affairs, his magnetic influence is more and more losing hold of a society immersed in business and distracted by a thousand interests. As a single person, he has not power to command, convince, or persuade. We can regard him now only as a symbol of that noble, heaven-born, celestial humanity which is always at work endeavoring to subdue the world to itself.

This *humanity* is the suffering Christ. It is he that teaches, toils, sorrows, pities, bears the buffet, submits to the scourge, carries the cross, glorifies the golgothas. As with the Israelites, the Messiah, "without form and comeliness," "despised and rejected of men," "the man of sorrows acquainted with grief," was not an individual, but the little united band of faithful Jews, so with us, the Christ who initiates the work of reconciliation between the extremes of mankind is the loyal company of the servants. It is they who live and die in hope to bring the race back to its unity, and so effect a reconciliation between the lower elements and the higher. Earnest men will one day speak of the need of this atonement, and of the efforts of this Christ to complete it, as powerfully and pathetically as Paul or Augustine spoke of the need of reconciliation with their Christ and the benignity of their Lord from heaven.

The apparatus of the atonement has been in some good degree completed. The outward appliances, the enginery, the mechanism, we see at work. Social arrangements have attained a considerable perfection. Modes of intercourse and communication are multiplied and organized. Networks of iron rails weave states together. Numerous lines of steamships keep up incessant concourse between the most distant shores. The telegraph annihilates time and space. Trade consolidates interests. The influences of law and civility are felt in all places. International treaties extend international obligations. The aspiration is everywhere towards unity. But suppose that this species of aspiration were far more nearly satisfied than it is, would the problem of atonement be solved? Will any amount of machinery, any amount of apparatus and appliance, be a substitute for the moral element, or perform the part assigned to it in the organization of society? Will railways convey us to heaven? Will

submarine cables serve as moral heart-strings?
Will the interlacing of interests create a holy
family, or the full recognition of the truths of social science establish practically the kingdom of
God? Has not emotion, feeling, sympathy, faith,
still a great work to do? Is the contagion of
earnestness to pass for nothing? In a word, is
the moral element to be wholly ruled out, and is
an enlightened selfishness to take the place of the
spiritual laws, displacing the bibles by some
" Poor Richard's Almanac," and ruling out the
prophets, exemplars and saints in favor of political economists and boards of trade? It may be
so; but I, for my part, still cling to my faith in
moral forces. I am persuaded that they work
outwardly from the centre, and that, but for them,
the very machinery we devise would not have been
invented.

For back of all these appliances, and through
them, works that ancient power, divine, human,
that power of earnest longing and love of which
Jesus is an illustration, and of which the " Christ "
has been the symbol. The old myth of a god
descending to the earth is full of suggestion still.
For, if we consider a moment, we are amazed to
see with what steady power, what tireless patience,
what implacable good-will, the pure elements of
human nature work, and have from the beginning
worked, to improve the condition and redeem

the state of mankind. The history of every invention is a story of almost incredible toil and consecration. Not the great exemplars of kindness merely, not only the world-renowned philanthropists, reformers, teachers, founders of faiths, missionaries, discoverers, prophets, martyrs to high ideal truth, men of genius, men of faith who have become centres of regenerating power, but the patient toilers and discoverers of every kind compose the company of the redeemers. Comte's Positivist Calendar devotes each day in the month to the name and memory of one of these saviours, copying the saints' days of the Roman Church. What a list of names it is, and what a store of energy and creative force it suggests! Thirteen months of days, and for every day a working man! The calendar of the church is thin and bloodless beside it. The lives of the saints make very dull reading, dry, monotonous, exaggerated, fantastical, repulsive, a tiresome pounding on a single string, which has little resonance and less music; but these lives are rich in sympathy and variety. Study the history of the steam engine, the magnetic telegraph, the sewing machine; go into the roots of the matter, trace the line of the discoverers, improvers, perfecters, back to the beginning; see what crosses they bore, what deserts they wandered in, what stripes they endured. Take up the biographies of Watt or Fulton, of Morse or Stephenson or Elias Howe,—they are romances of single-heartedness and denial. Our simplest tool and most familiar instrument of service cost the precious life-blood of one or more men, the latchet of whose shoes we are unworthy to unloose. Every improvement in labor-saving machinery, every plan of social organization, every effort at the rearrangement of civil or political conditions, every attempt at a re-adjustment of interests, every endeavor to reform an abuse, remove an obstruction, correct a mistake, mend a law, alter a custom, remedy an evil, has cost the very best life there is in humanity; experiment on experiment, failure on failure, discouragement on discouragement, sorrow on sorrow, the bruising, bleeding, breaking of the sweetest hearts that beat. There have been hundreds of Gethsemanes, scores of Calvarys. You may make your heart burn any day by dipping into the experiences of the men and women who have done but a small share in the work of overcoming the obstacles that lie in the way of reconciliation. The legend is not written in the New Testament, it is written in numberless books and pamphlets, reports, magazines, newspapers, that every one can read; the air is warm with touching appeals which, if they could be heard, would soften the hardest heart.

If the day-laborer could recognize and feel the

beneficence of the minds that invented the labor-
saving machinery that he dreads and destroys as
an enemy, his bitterness of hate would subside,
and he would cease to fly in the face of his best
friend. If the artisan, forgetting the apparent
discord between himself and the man who employs him, could be made to appreciate the accumulated treasure of patient heroism expressed by
that hated word " Capital ;" if the unlettered could
be brought to understand the ineffable tenderness
involved in the sciences and literatures which
wear such an awful aspect to them ; if the vicious
could have their eyes opened to the benignity of
the virtue they are daily outraging and crucify-
ing ; if the criminals could be induced to regard
the law that watches, restrains, punishes them, as
the redeeming thing it is ; if the sinful could have
it borne in upon them that the social order they
regard as their persecutor, their tyrant, their tor-
mentor, is in truth their best friend—that the
very tenderness of heaven is in it, that their turpitude and baseness is that of a child that
should strike its mother,—the tough old heart
would begin to throb and bleed again. The observation of life shows that people are still much
more governed by their feelings than by their interests, and surely the materials for working on
the feelings are here abundant enough. If one
tenth part of the pains were taken to use them

properly that have been taken to make effectual the sufferings of Jesus, the power of consecrated life would be felt on an immense scale, and conversions would increase in sincerity as well as in number. Every good man does something after his kind to abolish hate, mitigate suffering, assuage sorrow, confirm nobleness. Every useful man is a reconciler; every true, honest and pure man is a minister of peace; all sacrifice is atoning sacrifice, for it helps to draw together the alienated.

All atonement, says the church, is by blood. "Without blood is no remission." The Redeemer shed his blood on the cross, and the followers of the Redeemer have in all ages borne their crosses, leaving bloody foot-tracks on the soil of history. And blood answers to blood; the god dies in order to effect his junction with the wicked world; wickedness dies in order to effect its junction with the god. The blood-offering, voluntarily or involuntarily, is the law. Judas expiates his sin by self-murder; the criminal pays his forfeit on the gallows; the man of violence meets with violent death by accident, poison or the dagger; the apostate people perish by war; the nation that has shed innocent blood of Coolies or Africans must pour out the blood of its own children at Antietam and Gettysburg.

This is the church doctrine. What shall we say

of it? This: atonement is by blood, but not by
the shedding of it; rather by its saving and puri-
fication. Phlebotomy is no more to be applaud-
ed in theology than in medicine. Infusion, not
effusion, is the word. Blood means life; it is the
symbol of love, exuberance, joy. But life and
love and joy are all augmented by sharing. The
more you spend them the richer you are. The
sacrifice of Jesus was simply the voluntary, glad
outpouring of his fullness, and all sacrifice is of
the same quality. The crucifixion of Jesus in
history was an untoward interruption of his life-
bestowing career, a cessation of his loving influence, the stoppage of his regenerating heart-
beats. Judas would have better expiated his
fault by living to mend it. The murderer would
make more complete atonement by useful labor.
Reconciliation is effected by co-operation of service. Set the blood flying in this way; make
all people feel that they are of "one blood," and
the true at-one-ment will be finished. Let the
cross mean, not the painful surrender of life, but
its glad overflow; wipe from the altar the spots
of gore, wash white the priest's bloody robes, pu-
rify the halls of divinity with disinfectants to remove the cadaverous smell, revise the theological
death-code, purge the vocabulary of its ghastly
words, disenchant the emblems, lay stress on the
sympathy not the suffering, and the old problem
will receive a new solution.

VI.

POWER OF MORAL INSPIRATION.

MR. LECYK, at the close of his powerful and eloquent book on Rationalism in Europe, in which he traces with conscious superiority and hardly concealed triumph the progress that reason has made in the fields of practical and speculative thought, and celebrates with pride the successive victories of intelligence over ignorance, prejudice, and superstition, falls into a strain of sadness as he reflects on the moral tendency of the very principle whose power he has so successfully vindicated. He regrets the decay of the old heroic ethics, the decline of the spirit of enthusiasm, the departure of the grand virtues of disinterestedness, magnanimity, sacrifice which distinguished the otherwise barren periods of history, and declares that in the course of our intellectual progress we have lost spiritual qualities of priceless worth. He deplores the mercenary, venal, prosaic character of our modern utilitarian age, the feeble action that men of genius or faith exert on the masses, the intimate connection between a philosophy founded on sensation, and a morality based on vulgar conceptions of interest. There is a touching eloquence in such a confession from such a man, so clear, consistent and brave ; and coming from such a man, it compels us to hearken to it. It may be true, though we doubt, that the nobler ethics are disowned ; that the lofty virtues of self-denial, generosity, magnanimity, loyalty to principle, devotion to high ideal aims, are passing into disrepute ; that " Common Sense," as it is called, in other words, the consideration of immediate personal interest, is taking the place of the fine inspirations of elder time.

Earnest people say they see this, and grieve over it ; regard it, if not with anxiety, at least with concern.

In our large modern world these fine qualities, always rare, are not conspicuous ; in our altered world they are more than overbalanced by the qualities that characterize a commercial age. But it would be easy to enumerate examples of the grandest type of character in our own age and even in our own matter-of-fact land, and the respect paid to them, the enthusiasm they inspire, the influence they exert, is evidence that the qualities they embody have not lost their hold on

mankind. The standard of character among those
who recognize a standard is as high as it ever
was, and there is no sufficient ground for fearing
that it will be lowered. Mr. Lecky's apprehension springs perhaps from a sentimental element
in his constitution which at times seems to be
morbid. He must have forgotten, when he wrote,
men and women in Italy, Germany, England,
who were keeping fresh the finest traditions of
classical and of Christian heroism; he could not
have remembered that such as they, were, even
in the choicest classical epoch, and in the peculiar " ages of faith," the distinguished exceptions
to the common rule.

But were what Mr. Lecky says perfectly true, it
does not follow that the alleged moral doctrine
ensues from the increase of the rational principle. For when that principle shall have been
clearly understood, and shall have finally tri-
umphed, it is fair to suppose that it will restore
whatever may seem to have been lost, and will
do complete justice to the whole nature of man.
When men act rationally, if they ever do, they
will act nobly. When they act in full view of all
reasonable considerations, not in partial view of
the few considerations that lie immediately about
them, they will rise to a loftiness of motive and a
dignity of conduct that will quite match the ancient standard in elevation, while surpassing it in

reasonableness. But that time is far enough from having arrived yet. They who live rational lives are the few. Few are they who take any but the lowest view of interest. Reason is thus far excessively weak as compared with passion. The animal instincts are still so strong as to require perpetual curbing. We see daily examples of the extreme difficulty that even able men, favorably situated, elegibly circumstanced, well endowed, responsibly placed, with encouragements and incitements to virtue all about them, have in controlling and subduing their inclination to do dishonorable things ; daily examples of the hopelessness of the struggle between judgment and instinct ; between reason, honor, affection, duty, and some degrading vice like intemperance and licentiousness. It is so hard to hold rational considerations in mind at all, for any length of time, so very hard to hold them against the weakest opposing force, so all but impossible to hold them against the desire for pleasure or profit when it sets in strong upon even fairly-balanced minds, that it must be very long indeed before the average of mankind will submit to this mental, ideal, purely invisible and impalpable control. Reason has its development yet to gain. Even the simplest knowledge of the simplest laws, the laws of physical health for instance, the laws of relationship between obvious interests and familiar groups of circumstance, comes very slowly and is very slowly diffused. The knowledge that co-ordinates facts, rests on wide generalizations, covers long reaches of time and space, is much rarer ; its progress is hardly appreciable ; its spread can scarcely be traced ; its influence is too small to be estimated. And yet on the increase, nay, on the prevalence of this, the maintenance of purely rational morality must depend ; so long as this is absent, so long as the impulsive, passionate element is supreme, so long will some special inspiration to noble sentiment in action be necessary. Passion can be resisted by passion alone, impulse must be set against impulse, desire must counteract desire, feeling must operate against feeling ; a tide of enthusiasm must swell and overbear the tides of appetite. And in an age like ours, whence shall this enthusiasm come ?

We must look for it still from religion, and in order that religion may produce it, there must be some new interpretation of its great teachings.

Hitherto in Christendom the source of moral inspiration in the multitude of mankind has been the personal Christ. High spirits have drawn from higher springs. Some exalted souls in and out of Christendom have been filled and fed from the perennial fountains of their own abounding hearts. Their beautiful visions have been interior ; on the throne of their private conscience sat their inspiring deity. But the multitude of mankind have looked for moral support to the Christ alone. Let us never fail to appreciate the significance, or to do justice to the weight of that conception. It was a saving conception, a source of moral regeneration for centuries. Let us place it before us for a moment, and consider the elements of its power.

The vision of an absolutely sinless character ; this was the first element of a human being, circumstanced and conditioned like other human beings, sharing the ills of their mortality, like them exposed to poverty, hunger, fatigue, and whatever else miserable people in miserable times have put upon them, yet sweetly, patiently uncomplainingly, gratefully bearing it all; wounded without crying, deserted without hating, tempted without falling, his life a perpetual rebuke to all the rest of his fellow men, a miracle of human character yet made of the same stuff that the cheapest human characters are made of ; a standing reproach and a standing glory to the race; shaming the worst, illustrating, confirming, immortalizing the best that humanity is capable of ; this was the first element of power in this marvellous conception ; an imaginative conception, mainly, an ideal as we say, but somehow so artfully associated, so intimately identified, in fact, with an historical person that its entire reality was not, could not be, doubted.

This being, so transcendently fine, so godlike, so exempt from mortal responsibility, it would seem, lives, toils, dies, not in the pursuit of riches or power or fame, but that the lost of his kind, those with whom he could have no natural sympathy, those who must have been disagreeable, repulsive, loathesome to him, might be rescued from their worse than wretchedness. He sets an example not of goodness merely but of disinterested, devoted, self-sacrificing goodness. The lesson of his character and career is not " do as you would be done by," but " do as humanity prompts," " live for others," cast every form of selfishness aside, never think of yourself at all, not even of your spiritual self, not even of your soul, but give up all you have and are to the well-being of your fellow creatures. Make no account of suffering; reckon death as nothing in consideration of their need. " The son of Man came not to be ministered unto, but to minister and to give his life a ransom for many." " Being in the form of God, he made himself of no reputation, took on himself the form of a servant, humbled himself, and became obedient unto death." This is the second element of power.

One more step, and a most important one.

This being was not presented to mankind as a *historical* person, who lived indeed, but in the remote past; who was visible, but through the mist of ages; who toiled, and wrought, and suffered, but hundreds of years ago; who died, but had long been in peace. He was presented as a still existing, a still living, feeling, working, sympathizing person, glorified but compassionate, heavenly but present, sitting at the right hand of God, but none the less watching with interest deep as ever the conduct of those for whom he bled—the perpetual Saviour, the constantly thoughtful, anxious, encouraging, rebuking, regenerating Christ. Let that thought sink in.

Finally, and in this point the whole conception culminated, this being was thought of and believed in as the Judge who at the last day would mount his throne, collect the nations around him, summon individuals one by one to his bar, place their lives before them in full review, pass sentence on them according to their obedience or disobedience to his Law, and consign them over to their merited doom.

This Christ, I beg it to be remembered, was no dogma, no fancy, no speculation, but an image made palpable by every device of art. He was painted in fresco and on canvas; exhibited in his agony and his triumph; in his humiliation and his glory; he was carved in wood and

stone, and set up, in places of resort, at the cor-
ners of the streets, by the roadside, in all wild
and in all charming spots, in public buildings,
churches, halls of state, in private houses too,
where he could be seen at all hours of the day;
and these visible representations of him kept before the eyes of men precisely those traits that
most strongly excited their moral emotions. Music conveyed to the ear the same impressions
that art made on the eye. The mass was a drama as effective and touching as the great masters
of sound could produce. Ritual forms and ceremonies, altar services, prayers, confessions, creeds,
conspired to keep ever in mind the image of the
suffering Saviour.

Is it surprising that such a conception should
have produced an extraordinary effect? That it
produced no more is the wonder. Not its success in creating virtues of the heroic type, saintly virtues like those of St. Francis or St. Charles,
but its failure to make such virtues more common than at any time they were, is the matter for
amazement. How could people who had such a
conception as this before them, who believed
themselves watched by such holy eyes, who knew
that they must one day look straight into them,
who had the hope of that heaven-bestowing
smile, or the anticipation of that eternally with-
ering frown—how could people whose hearts were

thus directly and searchingly appealed to, fail to be generous, noble, self-denying, self-sacrificing ? What prevented magnanimity from becoming the law of average existence ?   The mental insensibility of the age prevented : the hardness, crudeness, brutality of the western world prevented. They were bloody ages, inconceivably bloody and brutal ; ages of cruelty, despotism, violence, barbarity unspeakable.   The men were moral pachyderms.   No ordinary rifle-ball would penetrate their tough leathern hides.   Moral ideas had to be rubbed into them with vitriol, burned in with caustic.   They had to be told that their sins crucified Christ afresh every day, and even then they would not repent, for the rush of their savage life carried away completely, as by a boisterous flood, the obstacles that the priests were able to oppose to it.   Their moments of reflection were like the cold gleams of the sun that shine fitfully through the cloud-rifts on a cheerless November day.   They do not warm the earth, and they make more terrible the gloom of the sky.

To this conception of the Christ is due any conspicuous virtue for a thousand years and more. But that conception for some centuries now has been steadily fading away.   With the decline of Romanism it has declined.   Protestantism has been impairing its force from the beginning.   It took away the carved statue ; it destroyed the bloody crucifix ; it removed the pictured canvas ; it left no visible sign or emblem of the being men had worshipped. It talked about him, indeed ; preached about him, dogmatized about him, made mental pictures of him, set him up in the shrine of thought. But the shrine of thought is neither kept open nor inviolate in uncultivated minds ; mental pictures are seldom vivid, and they rapidly lose color ; the perpetual preaching fatigues ; the continual talking and dogmatizing dulls the edge of the intellectual tools. Protestantism never did for the mind what Romanism did for the eye, it could not, for it lacked the materials ; it made no account of the sensuous element which predominated, and great account of the mental faculty, which was dormant. A more fatal step than. this Protestantism took when it introduced the principle of reason and went to work undoing all that faith tried to accomplish. The mind questioned the truth of the conception the soul was worshipping. The New Testament story was read, pondered, discussed. Criticism came in, the paint was washed off the image, the pigments scraped from the canvas. The difference between the historical Jesus and the mythological Christ was discovered ; the spell was broken ; the inspiration was gone.

No longer does the image of the Christ sway

the heart of Christendom or rule its conscience.
That is too plain for argument. The churches
are full of Christians on whose moral natures that
once venerable and beautiful conception has no
effect whatever. They do not feel the searching
glance, they do not dread the future presence.
He is not a living presence any more, but a
doubtful, dismembered, half-discarded dogma to
which no argument gives the semblance of reality. Their worldly lives catch no glory from
the clouded and rapi lly westering sun.

But it is the symbol, not the reality that has
disappeared. The real Christ remains, and possesses all the attributes that were ascribed to
the being whom Christendom adored. The true
humanity we have tried to set before us is
the Christ—the organized human elements, the
quality whereof our consciousness reveals to us,
the power whereof history and observation dis-
close. This Christ possesses all the virtues.
They are born of it. Jesus was one of its illus-
trations ; the heroes and saints are the flashing
out of its individual traits ; the philanthropists
are its active sentiments.

This Christ does indeed, as we have seen, live,
labor, suffer and die for mankind, setting a thousand examples of divine goodness. He dies daily, for no day passes without its history of hero-

ism, enacted perhaps before our own eyes, at all events within our ken.

This Christ is living, he lives always ; he is the same yesterday, to-day and forever, in every respect the same, only, if possibly ampler in spiritual gifts—wider in sympathy, richer in love, tenderer in feeling, mightier in purpose, sweeter in compassion than ever. He is the present lord, really present in the flesh and not merely in the spirit.

This Christ too, as has been said, is the Judge whose day is every day ; whom we must meet and do meet, before whose bar we stand hourly and are ranked either with the sheep or the goats.

Now why should not this conception have the same force with the other one that has played its noble part and had its victorious day, but has now left its seat of power? It is more real, more tangible, capable of as vivid a presentation to sentiment, feeling and conscience. Bring the moral nature close up against this conception and it cannot fail to receive a quickening thrill. For wrong-doing of whatever description under the form of vice or crime, social iniquity or broad inhumanity, implies a total unconsciousness of this living spirit of goodness, whether as exising potentially in the heart of the wrong-doer or as existing actually in the lives of noble men and women. Its disbelief is essentially in this humanity that the Christ symbolizes. The world is full of evil doers, and of evil doers who wear the garb of saintliness, who are sound in all points of belief, can quote proof texts by the score and argue down infidelity past answer; but the world has not yet seen a single wrong doer, whatever his type of transgression, who believed in the sanctity of his own simplest human relations. Nay, more than this, it has been observed that piety, so called, the ordinary piety of the Christian, by drawing the feelings away from these simple human relations, has left the door open to evil doing of almost every kind. The heart, gushing over with grief at the sorrows of an ideal man, has forgotten to pity real men : the conscience, exhausting itself in efforts to discharge its fancied duty towards a being who sate behind the clouds, has neglected its actual duty towards the being that sits on the door-step. Few have been more godless than some who have given themselves entirely to God ; few more christless than many who have been exceedingly jealous for the glory of Christ ; few more inhuman than those who have exalted Jesus to the skies. It is, I believe, an unquestionable truth that the most insidious and demoralizing kind of vice has been introduced into society and organized there and justified by people who had just passed or were about passing through a period of religious excitement, during which their affections were wound up to a pitch of ecstasy. In the name of religion they loosened the bonds of society; in the name of God they desecrated his temple; on pretence of keeping the perfect law of Christ they inaugurated a state of things that common people might characterize as vile.

Some forget the sanctity of human relations because their sentimentalism takes them high up into the clouds, and some forget it because their bestiality drags them far down into the mire. In either case the forgetfulness of *this human bond* is the cause of their evil doing. The breaking in on their minds of a conviction which the New Testament itself lifts to the rank of a religious belief would come like a revelation from heaven. Were this simplest of convictions to spread through our community now, that almost cant phrase, "The enthusiasm of humanity," would represent a feeling of the deepest and most over-powering description—a feeling that would carry people easily to heights of moral attainment such as the heroes of Christendom exemplified. Could this conception be put vividly before men, as it might be put by such eloquence as has more than once in Christian history swept multitudes away on the tides of enthusiasm, the chips and useless timbers and old stranded hulks that line the coast and choke up the river beds and block the bays of society abroad and at home, would be floated away or rescued for use; animal passion would receive a check. If some one could stop the throng of people whose idle, aimless, purposeless, vagabond existence is the danger, the misery, and the horror of our cities, and say to them: "Stay one moment and bethink you of what you are doing; you are throwing yourselves away; that perhaps is a small matter; if you could only die and be well rid of, the loss would be slight; it might be a nuisance well abated. If you were so many animals rooting in the mud, unconnected by sympathy with those about you, unrelated by organic ties to those before and after you—so that you went down alone—causing no ripple on the surface of the community—there might be little to say. Then drink on, gormandize, indulge, play the fool to the top of your bent; be a brute, and go the way of the brute. The sooner you kill yourself and make room for better men the better. But here it is; you are not alone; you are not unrelated; you are not your own master; in doing violence to yourself you do violence to a great many beside, and among them are the people who are trying to save you at their own great expense. One may strike at his own life and say: "Well, what of it? I don't care, my life is of no consequence; I am tired of it; let it end when and as it will, so it is

gay while it lasts. The future is too far off to
disturb me ; as for the immortal life, I know
nothing about it ; hell is an old woman's fancy,
heaven a young man's dream." Could we only
say then to such a one : " Very well, let that go ;
but, my friend, see this. In going down into the
grave, you carry more than a miserable carcass
back to its dust. You carry all that might have
been a useful, happy man ; the support, perhaps,
of others ; the ornament, possibly, of a circle ; a
source however humble, of influence and cheer.
The blow you strike falls heavily on some whom
you may see or may not see, but whom your every
movement affects as the light of a candle affects
every particle of matter in a room, or the stone
thrown into a lake affects every mile of the coast-
line. Look back on the long chain of those who
have gone before you, who have given you what
they had, and who have unconsciously staked on
you a portion of their hope. Look forward at the
long chain of those who are to come after you,
whose existence will in some mysterious manner
bear the trace of yours. Look about you, on
your kindred, your friends, your mates, the companions of your work or your leisure, the members of your circle or profession, fellow-citizens,
fellow-men, before whose eyes you walk, into
whose ears you speak, whose opinions you modify, whose motives you affect. By help of obser-

vation, reflection, imagination, memory, call these
about you, a brotherhood of fellow-creatures, a
vast family-circle, rich in sympathies, affections,
mutual responsibilities, cares, duties ; put yourself
in this line ; stand within this company ; then do
the base, the dishonorable, the inhuman thing, if
you can. *Drink* if you can, knowing that you are
dropping poison into these fresh veins ; *gormandize* if you can, knowing that you are loading
down the already too heavily-weighted intelligence, and clogging the already gasping will ; be
incontinent if you can, knowing that you may be
planting ineradicable disease in your children yet
unborn ; be *false* if you can, knowing that your
lie tears the fine web of mutual confidence that
holds communities together ; be *dishonest* if you
can, knowing that your fraud unsettles the very
basis of obligation and brings great houses with
a crash down upon humble roofs that shelter un-
suspecting families whose little all perhaps was
committed to hands they trusted would help them
and not destroy ; be *cruel* if you can, knowing
how in this world gentleness is the one most needed grace ; be *tyrannical and oppressive* if you
can, knowing that by so doing you break the
divine order of society which rests on the equal
rights and prerogatives of the human ; be *profane*
if you can, knowing that your blasphemy shocks
and insults the reverence whose holy awe gives

solemnity to all human feeling ; be *idle and careless* if you can, knowing that inertness and recklessness derange the action of those agencies on
which the social health depends ; be *extravagant*
if you can, knowing that you waste others' liveli-
hood, if not your own, and excite the appetite for
luxury in people who cannot afford to gratify it ;
be *stubborn, morose, and bitter* if you can, knowing
that you spread a gloom over precisely the spots
that need to be sunniest, the spots where tired
men and women stop to repose and gladden
their hearts, and where the innocent children
sport in their joy."

What an inducement does not this simple
thought of the human kinship afford to the cultivation of sweetness and light ! I truly believe
that if it could be made familiar and vivid, it
would have a wonderful power to paralyze the
evil arm, and steal the evil mind away, stationing
on either side of each living man and woman, an
angel of terror or of trust, that would prevent any
from straying far to the right hand or to the left.
It should be more powerful over hard, and coarse,
and brutal minds than the conception of the
Christ of the Christian Church ever was, or from
the nature of the case could be. For he was not
seen, except with the mind's eye, nor touched, except as a carved image, or a painted picture. His
actual suffering was matter of old history, and

his present need was less than nothing. But this Christ brushes against us in the street; nay, has his abode in our own home. His cry we hear, though we stop our ears to shut it out; his suffering we see, though we do not pause to look, but pass hurriedly by on the other side.

Modern philosophy reveals a law of social development that has a very intimate bearing on this question of moral inspiration. I refer to the law of evolution, the nature and scope whereof have been demonstrated past peradventure, and illustrated past the point at which further exposition is required. This law simply rivets the members of the human family together, making links of gold of the airy sentiments that were supposed to be ephemeral. In view of this law of evolution which makes of society an increasing organically developing creature, the significance of the moral element becomes very impressive. This significance lies in its rendering society *self-developing, self-organizing, self-evolving.* It compresses all power within the compass of human attributes, makes the race its own providence, its own reformer and saviour. Hitherto providence has been thought of as *superhuman.* The source of moral power has been considered as standing outside of the race, and sending down inspiration into it. Hence the responsibility of human progress rested with God. It went on as fast as he willed, and no faster ; when he willed, it stopped ; when he willed, it was turned aside ; he " raised up" deliverers, helpers, guides, saviours, and it was quite proper to wait till he saw fit to give them commission. If things went right, he had his tribute of praise ; if they seemed to go wrong, men submitted as they could, charging themselves with the perpetration of some nameless guilt, trying to appease the divine displeasure, but never investigating their own conduct, never taking hold to improve their own estate. In this view of things, it was impossible to convince people of their responsibility. The blame could always be thrown upon God, and as he was blameless, all powers were virtually held innocent. An impression of moral fatalism deadened the action of conscience. Bad men and good men alike said they could not help it. Weak men and strong men placed themselves in the same category, and allowed themselves to be rolled and tumbled along, pulled to and fro by invisible strings, a prayer occasionally breaking the silence, a cry to Jesus for pardon and compassion piercing the firmament, to be succeeded again by dumb submission impotent complaint.

To all this the discovery of the law of evolution puts an effectual stop. All the impelling powers are now seen to be concentrated in the race, a live organism, which grows by the use of its own faculties. If it fails to grow, it is through its own fault alone. Whether there shall be peace or war, rule or misrule, purity or corruption, justice or injustice; whether national treaties shall hold or not, whether republicanism shall succeed or fail, whether the State shall be loyal or disloyal, whether the city shall be governed by its higher or its lower class, whether the streets and sewers shall be sources of health or disease, whether pestilence shall be invited or warned off, whether virtue shall strengthen the citizens or vice shall weaken them, are questions that men must answer for themselves. There is no higher tribunal before which they can be carried; there is no super-human or extra-human will by which they can be dealt with. If things go well or ill rests with those who are commissioned to make them go.

This idea restores to man his moral faculties, gives him once more the stimulus to effort, bestows on him the right of indignation, and the privilege to praise. Who helps the evolution on, and who retards it? They who help it on help everything on; every member feels the thrill, every particle tingles with the glow. They who retard it keep everything back, cause depression in all parts of the system, and deaden the springs of life. All the healthily active are benefactors, whether they do much or little, organize a state or regulate a household, invent a sewing machine or faithfully use one, reform the institutions of a city or lead sweet and simple lives, negotiate a treaty or keep their private faith; found a system of education or successfully rear a single child.

> If done beneath these laws,
> E'en servile labors shine.

All the morbidly and unhealthily active are malefactors, whether they do much or little, kill a man or corrupt a principle, steal from a treasury or debase a sentiment, betray a trust or trifle with a feeling, waste others' lives by recklessness or waste their own lives by idleness. The springs of action are so delicate that a hair may disturb them. We can understand the passionate impatience with wrong-doers that they feel who have conceived this idea in all its force; we can comprehend their abhorrence, their denunciation, their furious assaults on the people who thrive on the lower appetites of their fellow creatures, the pimps and panders and drunkard-makers, the knavish politicians, the demagogues who batten on the miseries of their countrymen. And we can understand the enthusiasm with which benefaction is hailed whenever it is recognized—the public and general beneficence, which touches no private need in special, but seems to work for the substantial good of mankind at large. In celebrating a great achievement like the liberation of a state, the pacification of a nation, the abolition of an evil like slavery, men betray the instinct of humanity, which gives them common cause with the redeemed.

It is true that these feelings are apt to be carried to excess. Both the indignation and the praise are often extravagant, overdone in expression, if not misdirected in their object. The bad are not so bad, nor are the good so good as they are painted. The benefactors and the malefactors get confounded. The wrong heads are broken, and the wrong heads are crowned. But these evils are incidental and correct themselves. Those who have been in the habit of thinking that God kept caldrons boiling and sulphur pits smoking for people whose only fault was ignorance or torpor, and had gardens of perennial flowers to crown people whose only merit was being piously born and credulously inclined, can scarcely be expected to become all at once reasonable when they themselves are the judges and the executioners. Fanaticism does not so easily die out. False standards of judgment and false standards of doom, exaggerated sentiments and overstrained passions, will be the rule for many a day; fire-brands will be flying about indiscriminately and garlands will be promiscuously distributed. There will be a good deal of mock-thunder and lightning, individual reformers will assume to be omniscient and will undertake to deal damnation round the land, modestly taking for granted that their seat is on the white throne and that their tongue's edge is the dividing sword. But it is the tendency of faith in the law of social evolution to reduce this excessive excitement within reasonable limits. For evolution proceeds slowly, step by step, and the judgment-seat is not in heaven above our heads, but on earth at the rear limit of possible attainment; and men must be taken for what they are, not for what they shall become; men cannot be judged to-day as they will be a thousand years hence.

For the rest, the purpose in the long run excuses the mistake. The sympathy, the wish to do something, the admitted feeling of responsibility, the hope, the endeavor to improve the working machinery of society, the recognition of the fact of a general movement onward, along a broad highway towards certain definite results, the clear conviction that some things assist the movement and that other things retard it—all this, with the pure moral influence that goes along with it, reduces the incidental error of the rational reformer to small dimensions. If the law of evolution—that and no private fancy or passion of his own—is his study and his guide, his moral pressure will impel men forward more than his errors of apprehension will keep them back. There is no danger that the law will work out its results too fast.

Is it said that we are the passive as well as the active agents of evolution, that the law trundles us along whether we will or no ; that brakes are as important as engines ; that vice plays its part as well as virtue, indifference as well as zeal ; torpor and turpitude as well as enthusiasm and heroism, and so moral distinctness are obliterated ? Let it be replied that the engines are as important as brakes, and rather more so, seeing that brakes are secondary and engines primary, and that the train itself acts as a perpetual brake rather more than sufficient in ordinary cases, except where there is necessity for a sudden stop, as in the law of evolution there never is. The natural inertia is check enough ; I hear Judas plead his merit, arguing that he should be blessed instead of execrated, because but for him the world might have been defrauded of the benefits of the redeeming death. The plea is not accepted. There was plenty of weight in the scale against Jesus without his. No man ever deliberately assumed the position of brakesman who was qualified for the position of engineer. They who elect at all, elect to be among the helpers, not among the hinderers. They who have humanity in view, have in view its progress. Whether reason or feeling be strongest in them ; whether as philosophers they watch the gradual march of improvement and lend their aid calmly, or whether as sympathizers they enter keenly into the miseries that afflict mankind, and work earnestly to remedy them, the finest inspiration comes from the thought that the march of improvement may be hastened, that the miseries may be alleviated. The thought is no less convincing to the head than it is kindling to the heart ; it seizes on philosophers like Stuart Mill and Herbert Spencer equally with enthusiasts like Victor Hugo and Joseph Mazzini ; on minds like Thackeray as powerfully as on minds like Dickens. It begets a heroism of reform, a devotion of philanthropy among members of the English aristocracy, and men of the working-classes. It appeals with the force of religious conviction to the people who have forsworn religion ; to secularists like Holyoake and positivists like Bridges. Nearly all the moral enthusiasm of our times bears the stamp of this belief. The popular phrase " The enthusiasm of humanity " implies it ; a phrase that is open to criticism on several grounds, and is particularly objectionable as leading the mind away from reasonable considerations, and suggesting the reproduction, under another name, of the inconsiderate passion for Christ that led

so many astray. Such enthusiasm is a thing to
be deprecated, but its existence, or the attempt to
call it into existence, proves the strength of the
idea we have been developing in its ethical direction. That there is danger in it has been illustrated by no one as startlingly as by August
Comte.

In Comte's opinion the Golden Rule is defective in being egotistical in spirit. " Whatsoever
ye would that men should do unto you ! " Self reference then is the ethical principle ; self gratifica-
tion the ethical motive. The " Religion of Humanity " demands, in his judgment, a human law,
by which selfishness shall be under every form rebuked. This law the French philosopher expresses in the formula, " Live for others." According
to him, self-abnegation must be as complete as it
ever was in the ages of Faith. " All honest and
sensible men," he says, " of whatever party, should
agree by a common consent to discard the doctrine of rights. Positivism recognizes only duties." There is the old fanaticism again ; the one-
sided, one-legged principle, that cannot walk or
even stand upright, to escape from the evils of
selfishness. He abolishes the principle of self-
love ; he annihilates individuality, that the ex-
cesses of individualism may be abated. It is like
killing the man to avoid the distant danger of his
perishing by disease. But individualism is as

precious as universalism; suicide is no more respectable than murder. Not egotism, not altruism, but, to make another abominable word, relativism. The relation between the two is the momentary thing to be considered. The beauty of the law of evolution lies in its power to secure both. By its graduation, its slowness, its ever steady march, its firm conditions, its demand for thoughtfulness, carefulness, judgment, it discourages the heat of passion, and for enthusiasm substitutes earnestness, for fanaticism fidelity. It keeps the individual in his place, and holds him to his duty there, and decrees it the most solemn part of his duty to make strong and bright the special link in the human chain which he represents. The Golden Rule has the merit of reconciling perfectly self love and brotherly love—the ego and the new ego. It makes self love the basis of charity and charity the interpreter of self love. But the Golden Rule is defective in that it makes personal feeling the criterion of moral duty. A safer rule than Compte's would be "Live for the whole;" live so that the relation between you and others may remain unbroken ; that the currents or active sympathy may flow evenly on ; that your life may fit firmly into its frame, and deposit its contribution just where it belongs. Do your best according to intelligence and ability, as the minute hand does its best in the clock. Neither selfish nor unselfish, but meeting the requirements of both by fidelity. The more each makes of himself the more he contributes to the whole. The more he contributes to the whole the richer he becomes himself.

VII.

PROVIDENCE.

THE being of God implies providence. Through providence we feel our way back to being; the indications of care point to the care-taker. The notion of providence is as universal as the notion of Deity. " All things are full of Providence," said the Emperor Marcus Aurelius. The Hebrew Scriptures celebrate providence in every form of speech. Historian, poet, moralist, prophet, song-writer, delight in expressing in characteristic way their conception of the divine superintendence. The Jewish people themselves are considered in their history and literature as furnishing the most convincing proof of it. Providence is the theme of the bible. Jesus says: " Not a sparrow falleth to the ground without your Father." The poets, ancient and modern, prose writers too, bear witness to the general, we may say, the instinctive belief in a great Care over the world of things and men. It may be doubted whether the belief is ever absent from the human mind, or can ever be eradicated. Walt Whitman, in his strange fashion, but with more than his usual power, lifts up the psalm to providence in his "Faith Poem."

I do not doubt but the majesty and beauty of the
    world is latent in any iota of the world ;
I do not doubt there are realizations I have
    no idea of waiting for me through time
    and through the universe.
I do not doubt that temporary affairs keep on and
    on, millions of years ;
I do not doubt that the passionately wept deaths
    of young men are provided for, and that the deaths of
    young women, and the deaths of
    little children are provided for ;
I do not doubt that shallowness, meanness, malignance are pro-
    vided for ;
I do not doubt that whatever can possibly happen
    anywhere, at any time, is provided for, in the inheren-
    cies of things.

This is the language of faith. Faith sees no difficulty in supposing a foreseeing, forecasting, forefeeling deity; indeed it cannot rest in any other. Faith wants a bosom to lie upon, a hand to touch, a divine form to embrace, a celestial countenance smiling or pitying, a heavenly eye glancing kindness or dropping tears. But the intellect hesitates to authenticate the assertion. As Diderot said : "The lesson is in Hebrew ; the heart can comprehend, but the mind stands too low for vision." Henry Alabaster reports a dialogue with a modern Buddhist who argues thus : " The Brahmins and other believers in God the Creator believe that he makes the rain to fall that men may cultivate their fields and live ; but it seems to me that if it were so, he would of his great love and mercy make it fall equally all over the earth, so that all men might eat and live in security. But this is not the case. Indeed in some places no rain falls for years together ; the people have to drink brackish water, and cannot cultivate their lands ; besides, a very great deal of the rain falls on the seas, the mountains, the jungles, and does no good to man at all. Sometimes too much falls, flooding the towns and villages, and drowning numbers of men and animals ; sometimes too little falls in the plains for rice to be grown, while on the mountain tops rain falls perpetually through seasons wet and dry." Faith in providence has to meet severe shocks when thus confronted with facts enormous in magnitude and almost numberless in kind ; unfed hunger, unclothed nakedness, unsheltered weakness, unprotected gentleness, unconsoled sorrow, wasted products, squandered life. The vindications of providence in the usual sense, overlook these apparently uncared for wildernesses of the world, and fix their attention on some particular spot where the divine thoughtfulness has seemed to break visibly forth ; some individual experience which has been peculiarly favored ; some striking instance that seemed to reveal the guiding hand.

An eminent Christian writer, to make the matter plain, suggests that providence steadily keeps the Christian religion in view. "It is not the nations," he says, "but the Church that God has cherished as the apple of his eye. Towards Calvary, for thousands of years, all the lines of history converged, and now, for other thousands of years, to the end of time, will the lines diverge from Calvary till the kingdoms of this world have become the kingdoms of our Lord." This explanation, which seems to be quite satisfactory to the orthodox divine, implies that the deity is orthodox, and is chiefly interested in the prevalence and establishment of evangelical doctrines.

But was not the Canaanite a child of God ? Is not the Turk a man and a brother ? By what title does one religion monopolize providence in behoof of its own members ? And when Romanist and Protestant quarrel over their respective claims to the divine forethought, can anything be more ludicrous than the assumption that either has the exclusive use of God ? A care that extends to less than all humanity an equal kindness is certainly not heavenly. A partial providence —Semitic, Aryan, Mongol, Gallic, Slavic, Teutonic, Celtic, Saxon, Anglo-American—is none. No

tutelar deity is God. A providence that gives to
Prussian King William the victories he fights for,
that throws its dice with the heaviest battalion,
is considerably less than human or even European in its scope. Is providence to be credited
with the terrible military system of Prussia, or
with the crafty statesmanship that struck the bell
when the hour of war had come ?

The conversion of Paul is claimed as a clear
proof of immediate providence in human affairs ;
but the Jew might say that the providence rather
showed itself in the bonds, imprisonment, ship-
wreck and bloody death that befell the apostate,
and were the doom pronounced by heaven on his
crime,—the conversion being incontestably a per-
version.   Luther took as a special providence in
his own behalf his singular escape from the lightning bolt that struck down the companion who
walked by his side. But what would his companion have said had the other man been blasted ?   Or what did the friends of the companion,
who perhaps were Romanists, say to it ? Does
providence care so much more for Luther than
for another, that it matters not if the other be
shrivelled, so Luther be saved ? A friend with
much earnestness repeated to me the story of a
remarkable deliverance from death. He had engaged passage on a steamer from San Francisco to New York. On the day before sailing, a

strong mental impression—a sudden foreboding of evil—induced him not to go in the steamer, and he staid behind. The steamer sailed. Between San Francisco and Acapulco the boiler burst. The vessel sunk and a great many people perished. What shall we say of the providence that saved one not particularly valuable life and allowed a score of lives at least as valuable to be lost? Did a special providence impel the others to embark? Many a steamer narrowly misses collision with the iceberg, and the passengers give thanks for their miraculous deliverance from death. The Arctic comes along at the fatal moment and rushes into the frozen monster's embrace. Why should the one vessel keep the deadly appointment with the ice-mountain, and the rest keep their friendly appointments with the shore? Why should God have selected that particular ship for destruction? If it be a providence that rescues this boy from drowning when the Sunday excursion-boat is capsized by a sudden squall, it is a providence that drowns his comrade. If there be a providence in the safe arrival of one railway train, there must be a providence in the pitching of the next one down an embankment. Could we prove that all the people in the first train were saints, and all the people in the last train were sinners—that all the saved were orthodox Christians, and all the mangled and

slain were heretics, infidels and atheists ; did it
appear that the saved thenceforth led better lives
—there would be a clue to the providential character of the event.   But this never can be shown.
The saints are as often lost as the sinners ; the
sinners go on sinning as gaily after the deliverance as they did before.

A providence without *intention* is no providence ; if the intention completely eludes discovery, it is impossible to tell what or where the
providence is. Care implies thoughtfulness, and
acknowledged care implies thoughtfulness mani-
fest and appreciated. A capricious and imperfect
providence does not meet the demand either of
intelligence or faith : and providence seems capricious and imperfect, unintelligent and purposeless,
as soon as our eyes are lifted from the immediate
occasion that interests us to a general survey in
which others besides ourselves are comprehended.

To say that providence is incomprehensible
is no answer, for that merely puts questioning
off. If it is utterly incomprehensible, nothing can
be affirmed or denied of it ; we cannot even say
that there is any such thing. Some clue to it,
some key, some hint of its method, aim, purpose
a segment however small of its circle, must be
given before the baldest idea of it can be formed in
the mind. The divine foresight must have something in view, the divine forethought must contem-

plate an object : the divine feeling must tend towards definite end, else affirmation concerning them is out of the question ; and whether we take a broad survey of things about us, or we run our thought over long reaches of space or time, our clue is completly lost.

Mr. Beecher says : " All the events of life are precious to one that has this simple connection with Christ of faith and love. No wind can blow wrong, no event be mistimed, no result disastrous. If God but cares for our inward and eternal life, if by all the experiences of this life, he is reducing it and preparing for its disclosure, nothing can befall us but prosperity. Every sorrow shall be but the setting of some luminous jewel of joy." Yes, but that " if !" Can it be shown that God does care for our inward and eternal life, that all the experiences of this life are preparing for its disclosure ? Are men really nobler for their suffering, sweeter for their sorrow, finer for their discipline, richer for their losses, more heavenly minded for their earthly disappointments and defeats ? If they are, why do they not show it ? If they are not, what becomes of the providence ? God must certainly accomplish what he purposes ; and if he purposes to make men and women christians and saints that will be evident to all eyes. Our faith and love will be part of his ordinance. It will not be for us to bring the transmuting efficacy that is to convert evil into good. He that provided a Saviour for human sin, must he not also provide hearts to give the Saviour welcome? To say that we must furnish the strange alchemy that turns the baser metals into gold, is saying that we are the providences, that the universe is but raw material, which we are to work over as the shell-fish work the sunshine millions of miles off into the iridescent lines of its pearly coating; as the lily works into its convolutions the currents that circulate in the air.

Thus logic and observation beat the personal and special providence off the ground. The conception of an infinite Being, who picks out states, tribes, individuals, for peculiar favors; who looks in flowering bushes for a strolling Moses; waits beneath the orange groves of Damascus for a soul-tormented Paul; watches the moment when a hot-tempered Luther shall be found walking with a single comrade; loosens the rail at the precise instant that a special train passes; pushes down the iceberg in season for this or that steamer; a conception of God as Romanist, or Calvinist, or Unitarian, Theist, or Pantheist, is too irrational for philosophy. The aspect of a world incomplete, unregulated, unblessed, a world in the throes of struggle, unable as yet to find the thread of its own destiny, is discouraging to this idea.

Tho religious man cannot believe that the un-known and unknowable one is a polemic or a sec-tarian. The philosopher gives up the theory of final cause as inapplicable to a system regulated by universal and impartial laws. The man of practical understanding cannot believe that a world so full of wants is cared for in detail by a perfect intelligence.

Faith, however, falling back on fine generalities, refuses to abandon the problem, and science comes to the aid of Faith ; not of " the faith " of any church or sect, but of rational faith. Every indi-vidual reading of providence is dismissed as irre-levant, but the order of providence is asserted. The dispersion of the clouds reveals the firma-ment ; the removal of the scaffolding shows the proportions of the edifice. The whole universe, from mollusc to man, from star-dust to society, from the rolling and tumbling of the primeval fire mist to the revolutions in States, from the trans-mutation of carbon into diamond, to the transmu-tation of vice into virtue, is shown to be an or-ganism, every part of which belongs to every other part—a living, breathing, growing system, slowly evolving itself, expounding, developing, with a precision and symmetry that finds its sym-bol in the unfolding structure of the rose or the forest tree. In this organism everything has its allotted place. It could not but be where it is, or as it is. It was foreseen and fore-determined. Every pain, every sorrow, every failure, every success, every mistake, every just calculation, every false step, every true step, the thoughts, feelings, speculations, determinations of men, efforts, checks, impulses forward, draggings backward, actions, reactions, the ebb and the flow of moral purposes, the flash and sparkle of spiritual fountains, the sinking of water in the spiritual wells, everything comes by law, everything is under a divine necessity, strong as the ancient heavens, yet so tender that it will not brush the bloom from a rose leaf a minute before its time, or break the bruised reed with overweight.

Let there be no more talk of chance. The language of Tennyson is not too strong :

> " That nothing walks with aimless feet,
>   That not one life shall be destroyed,
>   Or cast as rubbish to the void,
> When God has made the pile complete ;
> That not a worm is cloven in vain,
>   That not a moth with vain desire,
>   Is shrivelled in a useless fire,
> Or but subserves another's gain."

Not a sparrow falleth to the ground without a cause for its broken wing or failing breath, a reason for its inability to use the inexhaustible buoyancy of the living air. There is a reason why this man takes the particular steamboat or

train, why the boy gives the fatal twist to the
rudder of his sail-boat, why this especial buf-
falo turns on the grand-duke Alexis, and is
killed, why this partridge of all others is snared,
why this member of the school of fish is caught
in the net, why this particular beetle or butterfly furnishes a specimen to the entomologist.
The leaves of the aspen, the needles of the pine
tree, are all numbered. The divine mathematics
are inappreciable yet even by the calculus that
predicts the movements and reckons the weight of
an undiscovered star ; but who doubts that the
laws of mathematics hold good in the unsurveyed
fields of creation ?

There is no such thing as luck. Luck is simply
untraced and thus far untraceable law. I once
knew a man with whom all things went awry.
Notwithstanding his utmost forethought and
pains, fortune never came to him. The train was
never on time ; the steamer always made the
long passage ; if a collision occurred, he was
there ; stocks invariably fell the day after his in-
vestment ; his venture always miscarried ; markets
were up when he had to buy, and down when he
must needs sell ; his gold was ever becoming
lead ; his diamond was ever being transmuted into
carbon. What was the matter it was impossible
to conjecture. There was a microscopic speck of
dust in the machinery ; some fine screw in the in-

accessible heart of the engine was loose ; there
was too much oil or too little, or oil of the wrong
kind. An indiscernible streak of disability ran
through the man's mental structure and made it impossible for him to touch the handle or find the
key. He could not adjust himself to his conditions. His neighbor had no such difficulty. Good
things came to him unasked ; advantages waited
on him and begged to be accepted; fairies did his
work while he slept ; he never met with accidents ;
was always at the right place at the right time ;
whatever he touched turned to gold. It was un-
accountable. He was not educated or trained ;
he had no fine ambition ; he lazed idly about ;
hated work ; loved pleasure. But these defects,
these moral vices, did not seem to throw him out
of the grooves of success, or render him less a favorite of the stern, unbending, remorseless necessity, which is the justice of deity. A deep organic
instinct of sympathy, though he did not know
it, and could not have understood the terms that
described it, guided him to his point.

It would sometimes be a relief to think that
there is such a thing as chance—that there is
another power playing among the affairs of the
world, traversing the dread highways now and
then, and breaking a path through the impenetrable thickets of law. It would be a relief to feel
that there is a small crevice through which an eye

of love may shoot a glance or drop a tear upon a
pitying face. There is too much providence, we
sometimes feel. The world is such a mass of
thought that there is no room for *thinking* ; such an
ocean of purpose that there is no room for *willing* ; such a torrent of tendency that there is no
volition ; such a compact system of acting and re-
acting that there is no opportunity for *caring* ;
such a magnificent arrangement of means and
ends, causes and effects, needs and supplies, that
the loving feeling has not an inch to move in.
The personal disappears ; you cannot even hear
the " rattle of the golden reins that guide the fiery
coursers of the sun.")

The complaint of too much providence is as bitter as the complaint of no providence at all. A
special providence, not the providence that is the
same to everybody, and therefore special to none,
is the demand ; evidence of immediate thought
of living will, of thoughtful, pitying love.

It is here that the human providence comes in.
The human providence supplements the divine.
It is the divine care applied. The human providence is as far as it goes a special providence, and
the special providence is human. Man is the
directly thinking, purposing, willing, loving God.
There is just as much active personal care in society as there is human care. It is only through
human qualities that we guess at divine. The at-

tributes of God are but a reflection on the skies of
the attributes of men ; and according as we think
of these, shall we think of those. The hope that
God will be better to us than men are, is simply
the hope that human qualities will vindicate themselves in the future ; but at present God seems no
better to us than men seem ; for the quality of
men, such as they are—are the only organized
moral forces we know. Our ideas of justice, goodness, kindness, tenderness, compassion, have not
been given to us ready made, dropped into us from
some heavenly source ; they have been sown by
ages of effort, and poor, infrequent, fluctuating
and precarious though they be, are the best representatives we have of celestial powers. Where
outside of the human family do we find practical
sentiments of pity, or gentleness, or forgiveness ?
We may *read them into* the aspects of nature.
The poet speaks of the general beneficence of the
sunshine ; of the wide benignity of the rain ; but
he only carries over to the celestial phenomena
his personal feeling. The sunshine has no sentiment of good will towards the landscape or the
farmer ; the clouds do not care whether their rain
falls on the salt sea-shore or the poor woman's
vegetable patch. We impute a sweet intention
to the laws that hold the world together ; but
they are unconscious of it. We give the morning
stars their song ; we furnish the speech which day

utters to day, and declare what wisdom night showeth to night. But for man there would indeed be no voice nor language, their speech would not be heard. " In reason's ear they all rejoice." It is the ear that interprets, yes! that frames the joy.

So far then as there is direct *foresight*, *forethought*, *forefeeling*, it is human. We cannot go behind the veil, we cannot look beyond our own faculties.

If now we glance at the resources of providence, the actual supplies that are used for succor, benefit, consolation, we find that they are altogether human-earned, possessed, accumulated by men. The food that satisfies hunger, the clothing that protects against cold, the wood for the winter's fire, the fire that burns the fuel, are all of human provision. The raw material is given, but one may perish in the midst of our abundance of raw material. Tons of wool on sheeps' backs would be useless without shears and looms; acres of the cotton plant would be valueless without the factory; forests of timber would be unavailable without the woodman's axe; rivers of water would be of no use without bucket or well; oceans of inflammable gas would be inoperative without flint and steel and the wit to strike them together. The ministry of labor, experiment, invention, this purely human ministry goes before any and all supply of human necessities. The farmer, the hunter, the fisherman, the botanist the chemist, the great army of explorers, experimenters, naturalists, are the agencies of the divine good will. Providence works' in the mill, toils in laboratories, sweats over the problems of social science, builds and excavates and dredges and bridges, and does its best to diminish the evils that infest mankind. The being that works hitherto and always is God, and the being that works hitherto and always is man.

The chief special agency of providence is *wealth*. Without wealth labor would cease, and the fruits of labor would not be forthcoming. The race would slowly die out and nothing would save it. Now wealth is peculiarly a human creation. The desire of it, the love of its possession, the eagerness to acquire it, the passion for keeping it, the means of increasing it, the institutions that make it effective are also human. Wealth does not drop from the skies ; it is not picked up on the ground, it is earned, created, by the industry and thrift of men. Where there is no wealth, there is no providence. If we could suppose a community in which there were none but poor men, no accumulated means, no gathered fruits of toil, providence it would be found, abandoned the care of that community. The people who gather or who hold from others' gathering this accumulation of resources, are, to the extent of that accumulation, providence. Carlyle says somewhere : he that has sixpence is master of the world to the extent of sixpence. With equal truth we may say : he that has sixpence is father of the world to the extent of sixpence. To that extent he provides for the needy, feeds the hungry, clothes the naked, employs the idle, beats off the gaunt wolf Want, ministers to the sick, the suffering, the dying. This sixpence trickles a thin silver stream over the fields of toil, sets mill wheels turning, cheapens food, opens iron mines and coal mines, floats merchant vessels and keeps full the channels of intercourse through which flow the regenerating currents of power.

Though the rich man be a miser, he is none the less, though unintentionally, a providence. Though he gives no mite to the poor, though he spends no dollar on institutions of public beneficence, though he encourages directly no industry, buys nothing to speak of at the shops, still he can no more help the ultimate effect of his accumulation than the cloud can help the discharge of its vapor in rain, or the sun the streaming forth of its beams, or the atmosphere the pressure of its density. The miser could not wholly neutralize the power of his providential agency, even if he buried his gold in an earthen pot, unless, indeed, the pot were so hidden that it could not be discovered. But if he invests it, as in these modern days he is pretty sure to do, (for the race of subterranean misers is about exhausted,) if he lends it out at interest to men who want to use it for the practical wants of society, it is at work all the time; it has a part in the development of new industries, in the employment of idle hands, in the achievement of great public works of general utility. It has a part in feeding many families, in supporting institutions of beneficence, in preventing sickness, lengthening the term of human life, promoting friendly relations among classes of people he had never heard of. He is a benefactor in spite of himself. While professing utter indifference to the want and suffering of the poor, cursing the beggar perhaps who comes to his door, turning a deaf ear to every appeal for charity, he may be dropping fertility on the distant prairies, and employing nurses in foreign hospitals.

Though the rich man be a spendthrift, he cannot wholly help being a providence, in as far as his wealth is concerned. He may not support the most desirable class of people, but he supports somebody. His sunshine may fall upon the evil, but that, according to the New Testament, is no condemnation ; and if his rain is sent to the un-just, we have the word of Jesus that its office may be heavenly. It is a good providence that helps' caterers and cooks, wine merchants and confec-tioners, dancers and lawyers, horse-breeders and carriage-builders, for all these people are men ; they have families to be provided for, children to be reared, doctors' bills to pay. It is not for us to determine what people have a right to live. God lets them all live. The talent may be a very small one, the service rendered very insignificant, but it is entitled to its reward. Nobody can be quite sure that he does the best thing with his money, and though we believe that the high-toned uses are the best ones, and that conscience, noble-ness, good will, kindness, have the duty as well as the right to make channels for the living stream, it cannot well be questioned that some people would do quite as wisely if they let the water run according to its own sweet will, and did not try to direct it according to their own misjudgment. Too much purpose is sometimes as bad as too little. Many a rich man thwarts his providence by excessive volition, being so very anxious lest his possessions should not go rightly, that he makes them go just where the natural laws would forbid. It is dangerous to try to control too ab-solutely what so many have an interest in, and more than one good man, with the best intentions to serve as a providence to his kind, has, through ignorance, diverted his wealth from its most effective and beneficial uses, more palpably than the spendthrift, who has let it run through his fingers and find its way by natural channels into society. I am speaking, of course, of the money, not of the men, of the material, not of the moral influence. The man with a generous purpose is a providence, where the man without a purpose is none. He ministers to the moral world, which the other serves not at all, but rather disorganizes. His rain and sunshine fall upon fields which the other neglects, or sows with tares, fields that produce, or should produce, the noble harvests of thoughtfulness, accountability, prudence, honor, and good will. But regarding the wealth alone, that will always feed somebody, and somebody to whom nature has given the right to be fed.

At all events, whether wisely distributed or unwisely, the distribution of all gifts is in human hands. Immediately, God distributes nothing. The almoner of all bounty, as well as the accumulator of all bounty, is man. The vast and various instrumentalities that supply mental necessities from bodily food to spiritual consolation, are in origin, plan, arrangement, mechanism, operation, human and human only. Man devised them, and man carries them on. Associations for the relief of poverty and misery, hospitals, asylums, houses of refuge, dispensaries, homes, schools, sisterhoods and brotherhoods of mercy, orders of nurses, physicians, consolers—in short, whatever from the earliest times till now has been meditated or achieved, thought, said or done to meet the occasions of mental need, has been in every respect human. No superhuman finger has ever appeared in it. Heart gifts come from the human heart; soul gifts from the human soul. It is man that offers friendship, sympathy, compassion, pity, counsel, help. Man succors, and man soothes. The prayer that uplifts, the conversation that quiets, the word that strengthens, the speech that reveals eternal beauties, alike proceed from human lips. It is man who lifts the burden of sorrow, care, or guilt, stills the heart, relieves the conscience, gives peace to the soul. This human providence has labored hard and patiently to meet every conceivable exigency. It is very wide, it is very powerful. It goes into the gloomiest places, it attacks the most discouraging problems. It is without fear or disdain; there is no bound to its thoughtfulness, no limit to its generosity, no stint to its good will. Its promptness and ingenuity and fertility of resource are wonderful. It will do things so delicately, with such modesty, such lightness of touch, such quickness of feeling, such nimbleness of intuition, that few suspect its agency, and the most are

persuaded that a special care from above inter-
venes.

George Muller and Charles Spurgeon, both
Englishmen, are persuaded that the Christ in
heaven supports their great orphan asylums in
response to their prayers. They are not, of course,
so wild as to imagine that the shoes and stockings visibly descend from heaven, that bread and
butter rains down, like the Hebrew manna in the
night time, that a celestial Santa Claus, whose
visits are not confined to the Christmas season,
puts caps on the children's heads, or that angels
drop charities which, on touching the ground, become barrels of fine flour. They know that the
flour is ground in a mill, that the stockings are
woven on a frame, that the shoes are made by a
cobbler, that the supplies are duly paid for in
shillings and pence and are brought to the door
in a cart; but the kind disposition that prompted
the donations, the considerate thought of the or-
phans—this, they believe, is sent into human
hearts in answer to their prayers. Such a theory
comes with a sufficiently good grace from men
who hold the natural depravity of human nature,
and are forced to ascribe every gentle emotion to
their ascended Christ; but such sensible, rational folks need not go so far in search of a providence so simple. That kindly people should hear
of an earnest work that was doing in their neigh-

borhood, particularly when it made such pretensions, is not surprising; that they should take an interest in it is just what might be expected; that they should be moved by their. hearts to help it on is by no means a marvel. More extraordinary things than that have been done hundreds and hundreds of times by this wide-awake, prying, gossiping, good natured, kindly, meddlesome spirit in men which delights in doing out of the way, far-fetched, eccentric, often indiscreet and foolish deeds of affection. Nothing more than human sympathy aided by human wit or witlessness is required to explain all that is done, or ever has been done to meet the touching sad occasions of human experience. Wherever there is help there is a human shape. There may be guardian angels—who has a right to deny it? but if there are they are simply human beings of nimbler foot, greater leisure, of ampler knowledge, who apply human remedies rather more deftly than spirits in churlier flesh can do.

We are all providences to more or fewer. Job said of himself, "I delivered the poor that cried, and the fatherless, and him that had no helper. The blessing of him that was ready to perish came upon me; and I caused the widow's heart to sing for joy. I was eyes to the blind and feet was I to the lame; I was a father to the poor, and the cause I knew not I searched out." Of how many another might precisely those words be said! of what ordinarily good man may not some of them be said. The kind father is a providence to his family, the tender mother is a providence to her children, friend is providence to friend, the employer is providence to those he employs, the mistress is providence to her servants. Who is so lowly as not to be providence to others of human kind? Every good act is providence; removing a stone from the path is providence; sweeping a crossing is providence; lifting one who has fallen is providence; putting a wanderer in the right way is providence; answering intelligently a question is providence; returning a pleasant look is providence, giving a cup of cold water may be a saving providence.

No providence is so human that it is not divine; no providence is so divine that it is not human. The most signal providences have a man behind them. The providence in the discovery of the American continent was the indomitable hope in the bosom of Columbus, and that hope was born of the spirit of adventure and discovery that pervaded the century and the land that gave him life. A whole group of divinities had their Olympus in that royal breast. No gem of the ocean could long elude the search of that searching hand.

This was the foresight that opened another world to what was then the greatest power on the planet. The providence that guided the May-flower, with its little company, across the wintry ocean—was the determination of those few men and women to face all perils and brave death itself rather than not find a home where their souls might be at peace. Their faith was their fore-sight ; the seeds of the harvest that was to feed the future New England and to sustain moral life at the extreme confines of the continent were stored up in the granaries of those trusting bosoms. The providence that brought on our civil war was the conscience of the North which forbade the utter sacrifice of liberty and resented the last insult of its foes ; and the providence that brought the civil war to an end was the constancy of the national will. Had that fal-tered, the dice of God would have decided against us. In the fullness of time " the man appears, the word is spoken, the deed is done : for in the fullness of time the man is nurtured, the word articulated, the deed meditated and pre-pared for. " As thy day so shall thy strength be," for strength is nurtured and trained by days of thought and endeavor, and at the proper moment, under the requisite strain, the thought culminates, the endeavor succeeds.

We complain of the inequalities of providence

but we must remember that providence, being human in special agency, though divine in spirit, shares the imperfection of its ministry. It has also the incompleteness of humanity. Defective it is and must be, because man is defective ; inorganized it is and must be, because man is inorganized. Human justice is all the justice there is ; consequently justice is but partially rendered. With human kindness and pity, such as they are, we must for the moment be satisfied, for they are all the kindness and pity we have. The infinite love finds as yet no human expression, which is only saying in other words, that it finds no intelligent expression at all. From age to age it has been organizing itself more and more effectively in society, but it is very far yet from an organization, complete, harmonious, effectual. The process of evolution still goes on. Resources are accumulating ; the application of them is becoming nicer, finer, fairer, day by day. The day will surely come when all needs will be satisfied, from the lowest to the highest, and the care we dream of and sigh for will be seen in the waste places, seeking and saving the lost.

VIII.

MORAL IDEAL.

REBUKING his disciples for their absurd ambition to get the best places in his kingdom, Jesus dropped one of those searching remarks that pack a philosophy into a paragraph. He said, "Ye know that they which are appointed to rule among the Gentiles exercise lordship over them; and their great ones exercise authority upon them. But it must not be so among you; but whosoever will be great among you shall be your minister; and whoso of you will be the chiefest, shall be the servant of all." The difference between two moral standards or ideals is here indicated with a precision that leaves nothing to be desired. Among the Gentiles, that is, among the Greeks and Romans in general, among the western nations the type of greatness and goodness, too, is the hero. He was the best who raised himself most above his fellows—who excelled in force, valor, wit, cunning, persuasion, beauty, in whatever quality made him master over human beings. The mastery was the merit. Prometheus, who outwitted Zeus, stole the fire from heaven, and, chained to Caucasus, bore the fierce tearing of the vulture's beak. Hercules, who killed the lion, slew the hydra, subdued the boar, cleansed the Augean stables, captured the Cretan bull, dragged Cerberus from the infernal regions; Perseus, who killed the Gorgon, and rescued Andromeda from the dragon, were deified and worshipped as models of prowess and patterns of success. They and their worshippers were of the race that believed in the individual, and cultivated the utmost possible attainment of self-reliance, self-will, self-exaltation.

Over against the hero stands the saint. Over against Hercules stands Jesus, who " came not to be served, but to serve ; and to give his life, that the many, the multitude, the man might be ransomed." He recommends and exhibits the utmost possible attainment of self-abnegation. He is the image of meekness, the model of patience. He makes no effort to aggrandize himself; he runs away from the crown—every crown but the crown of thorns ; he is dumb before Pilate ; he submits uncomplainingly to the scourge. He would not break the bruised heart, though it was the guiltiest, by another word of rebuke ; he would not quench the smoking flax of the flickering conscience by a single drop of discouragement. He washed his disciples' feet He had no shame in talking with the outcast, or in keeping company with such as were of no account. His peculiarity was an ever-present sense of the rights and claims of others. He had humanity constantly in mind. Out of humanity he spoke ; in humanity he lived. The individual with him was but member of a family, one of a brotherhood. The race from which he sprung believed in the power and the destiny of race. The thought of race was all in all to them. Their ideal man was the man who best represented his race, did the most to exalt it, carried its peculiar qualities to the highest point of eminence. We have a description of him in the 53rd chapter of Isaiah : "He was wounded for our transgressions, bruised for our iniquities ; the chastisement of our peace was laid on him, and by his stripes we are healed." Even David owed his fame not to his strength, or beauty, or kingliness, but to his recognition of the destinies of Israel.

In Jesus this sentiment of *solidarity*, of the organic unity among mankind, of mutual dependence and inter-dependence culminated. In him it was supreme. He always appeared as the representative of humanity, the "Son of Man." When he bade the adultress go and sin no more ; when he told the Magdalen to depart in peace, for her sins were forgiven her, he spoke not as

from himself, but in the name of the humanity
that he merely voiced for the occasion. When he
launched his invective at the Pharisees, and over-
whelmed the Scribes with his scorn, it was with
no individual feeling of anger, but with a mighty
conviction that the conscience of the nation, the
heart of the people, the soul of equity and kindness found utterance through his lips. " Say
what you will against the Son of Man," he cried,
" and it shall be forgiven. But he that speaketh
against the Holy Spirit shall not be forgiven."
" It is not I that speak." He claimed authority
on the ground that he better than any enunciated
the sentiment and declared the will of the Lord's
people. " Of my own self, I can do nothing : as
I hear I judge."

This image the Christian church set up for the
admiration of mankind. The lists of personal
virtues in the earliest literature of the church, all
bear testimony to the same kind of excellence.
Paul enumerates as the fruits of the spirit : " love,
joy, peace, long suffering, kindness, goodness,
faith, mildness, self control "—and as their opposites : fornication, covetousness, maliciousness,
backbiting, pride, disobedience, implacableness,
unmercifulness. He plants his peculiar virtues on
the same ground that Jesus took : *solidarity*,
membership in one another. " Let every man
speak truth with his neighbor ! " Why ? Be-

cause truth-telling is in itself admirable? Not
because "Ye are members one of another." He
recommends charity as "the bond of perfectness."
He is never weary of dwelling on the organic unity
of the believers, their membership in one body,
their spiritual partnership in one another, as
the final argument against pride, self-assertion,
assumption of superiority. "Let the same mind
be in you that was in Christ Jesus, who, though he
was in the form of God, did not think that our
equality with God was a thing he ought greedily
to grasp at, but made himself of no reputation,
and took on himself the form of a servant.

This moral ideal—the ideal of the saint, the
church of Rome adopted and exalted. The hero
was dropped. No sooner had it taken possession
of the imperial city of Rome than it proceeded to
substitute the idea of the god become a man, for
the idea of the man become a god. The statues
were removed or rebaptized; a cross, the sign of
self-crucifixion, was planted in the middle of the
vast arena where emperors celebrated their victories and gladiators fought with lions. It placed
the image of the Christ on the spot where before
had stood the image of Jupiter; the saint praying
for his murderers displaced the Hercules teasing
the Nemaean beast; the virgin with her babe in
her arms filled the niche once occupied by the
proud Diana or the disdainful Juno. The gods

and goddesses of the pagan world : Mars, the god of war ; Mercury, the god of traffic and cunning ; Bacchus, god of revelry ; Minerva, Venus, Ceres, were all supplanted by apostles, evangelists, martyrs, saints, who represented the very opposite qualities, peacefulness, temperance, simplicity, purity, faith, aspiration.

The fidelity with which the church of Rome adhered to its model was wonderful. It accepted none who did not conform to the conditions. It would not be bribed or persuaded or menaced into compliance with the pagan standard. It refused to accept the heathen ideal under any disguise. The saint was always the person who surrendered his private will. Humility, meekness, patience, these were the qualities she ever meant to canonize, and she never purposely canonized any others. The candidate for saintship might be a person of no outward consideration, of no social rank or degree ; he might be a slave, a beggar, a negro ; no matter. If he was proved to have possessed these qualities he received the crown and was lifted to the holy seat. The candidate for saintship might be a person of the highest position, rich, noble, great in fame. He might be a prince, a crowned king, a priest, cardinal, nay, a pope ; no matter. If he was not proved to have possessed the saintly virtues he did not receive the saintly name. The two most famous popes in history, Gregory

VII. and Innocent III. the two great vindicators of
Romish supremacy, are not enrolled in the list of
saints; for saints they were not. Humility and
meekness, simplicity and devoutness, were not their
virtues; and though the church owed everything to
their indomitable courage, their towering pride
and their far-reaching diplomacy, all these services availed nothing to class them where they did
not belong. There was here no distinction of persons whatever. There was one rule for all alike.
All must tread the narrow way into life. Humility made all kings. Pride made all subjects. In
its earthly policy the church was worldly minded
to a degree that would have scandalized a ruler
like Pericles or an emperor like Marcus Aurelius.
She truckled to power; was haughty when it
suited her purpose, and crafty when craft was
convenient. But in her final verdict on character
she was true to her master. She would allow only
the heavenly to go to heaven.

I do not say that she presented her moral
ideal in its noblest or completest form, round
and full, with no fine quality omitted or out of
place. This she certainly did not. Her model
was artificial and one sided. She allowed no
saintliness outside of her own pale, claiming to
possess a strict monopoly of the gospel graces;
and in logical accordance with this rule of
limitation, she refused to admit that these

graces were in any sense or in any degree an
outgrowth of human nature, the fruit of spontaneous spiritual activity, the natural product
of prayer and effort. She claimed the sole right
to manufacture them by her own machinery.
Is it any wonder that they had the stiff, hard,
angular, mechanical, done-to-order look that such
products always have? They were not "virtues,"
because the *vir* was left out of them; they were
not "graces," for ungracefulness was their characteristic. The one thing the Romish saint
lacked was the one thing that one cannot lack and
live,—blood. He was a sapless, nerveless being.
His humility was humiliation, his meekness was
meanness, his patience was passivity, his submission was subjection, his aspiration was breath-
lessness. He cherished no anger, for he had no
spirit. He loved the taste of dirt. It was easy
for him to forgive his enemies—for he did not
know what it was to love his friends. He set-
tled the whole question by making himself nothing. A sad, woebegone creature, without wants
or satisfactions, shy, joyless, dull in mind and
feeling, formal and austere, a creature of rules,
with a rope round his waist and a whip in his
closet, his eyes cast down or lifted up, never
directed straight before him, never looking frankly into other men's eyes, never studying curious-
ly the surrounding world. We see the same

type now in the hideous-looking men and women we meet in the street, priests or sisters of
Mercy, who think that by abdicating humanity
they resemble the Son of Man.

With Protestantism a new spirit came in, or
rather an old spirit revived. Protestantism was
simply the reappearance of the old heathen world
under a new shape. The revival of Greek and
Roman letters brought it in, and with the revival of Greek and Roman letters came the spirit of
Greek and Roman independence, the spontaneous,
exuberant, passionate spirit, the spirit of inquiry, of innovation, protest, reform, revolution, the
spirit that has made the new world. The moral ideal felt the force of this spirit early and
showed signs of modification beneath it. Other
elements began to appear ; humility, meekness,
patience, submission, peaceableness were not all
in all. There were bonds to be broken. There
was a despotism to be thrown off, a manhood
to be vindicated, a mind and heart and soul to
be set free. Passive qualities would no longer
suffice ; the negative side of human nature must
be supplemented by the positive side. There
was a reaction in favor of movement ; though
the word "progress" was not spoken, the breath
of progress was abroad and all who breathed at
all inhaled it. The hero came once more to
honor. Savonarola, one of the chief inaugura-

tors of the new era, stood midway betwixt the old and the new, combining the spirit of both. He was a mixture of hero and saint; Protestant and Romanist in one; a reformer and a believer; an agitator and a conservative; a defier of the Pope and a devout subject of the papacy.

Luther, his great successor, the man in whom the new spirit became incarnate, was a hero, no saint. He said of himself that he was "rough, boisterous, stormy, and altogether warlike, born to fight innumerable devils and monsters, to remove stumps and stones, to cut down thistles and thorns, and to clear the wild woods." Luther was a warm-blooded man, affectionate, friendly, kind, jovial, brimming over with humor, addicted to broad jokes, fond of nature and music, alive to all passionate delights. He had a vast deal of human nature in him, of all sorts, and he was not over careful to suppress it. He seemed the soul of self-assertion and self-reliance. He may have been as meek as Moses, but he was no meeker. His declaration at the conference of Worms, "No one can be compelled to act against his conscience. Here I stand; I cannot act otherwise; God help me. Amen!" was the shout of a hero to his hosts. "The song with which he entered Worms, followed by his companions, was," says Heine, " a true war song. The old Cathedral shook again at the strange sounds, and the ravens were disturbed in their nests on the top of the towers. This hymn, the Marseillaise of the Reformation, has preserved to this day the tremendous energy of its expression, and may some day again startle us with its sonorous and iron-girt words." There was not much meekness in the saying, " I·would make one bundle of Pope and Cardinals, and fling the whole into our little ditch of the Tuscan Sea ; such a bath, I pledge my word and back it with Jesus Christ as security, would cure them." There was not much of the temper of the peacemaker in the declaration, "the (insurgent) peasants deserve no mercy, no toleration, but the indignation of God and man." " The peasants are under the ban both of God and the Emperor, and may be treated as mad dogs."

And yet the stout soldier did pay sincere tribute to the evangelical standard. He fought not for himself, but for what he felt was the cause of God and man. In that cause he forgot himself. In that cause he was ready to die. In the conference at Worms he said : " I confess that I have been more rough and violent than religion and my gown warrant. I do not give myself out for a saint. It is not my life and conduct that I am discussing before you, but the doctrine of Jesus

Christ." Again : "It was my flock ; the flock entrusted to me by God. I am bound to suffer
death for them, and would cheerfully lay down
my life." " I myself no longer know Luther, and
wish not to know him. What I preach comes not
from him but from Jesus Christ. Let the devil
fly away with Luther, if he can. I care not, so
long as he leaves Jesus Christ reigning in all
hearts." "For me I neither am nor wish to be
master of any one. I and mine will contend for
the sole and whole doctrine of Christ who is our
only master." Here was genuine humility and
submission. Luther put tons of weight on his
feeling to keep it down ; at times he took himself to task for being too patient. He set himself
earnestly and sincerely in the background. He
fought no private battle, and rebuked himself
when it seemed to him that he might be putting
himself too conspicuously forward. He was under
law ; he served a master ; he made himself of no
account, for that master's sake. "I am only a
man ; I can but defend my doctrine after my
divine Saviour's example, who, when smote by
the servant of the high priest, said to him : "If I
have spoken evil bear witness of the evil." "I
pray you leave my name alone. Who is Luther?
My doctrine is not mine. I have not been crucified. St. Paul would not that any should call
themselves of Paul nor of Peter, but of Christ ;

how then does it befit me, a miserable bag of dust
and ashes, to give my name to the children of
Christ?" If the saint be one who surrenders
his will to the supreme will, then was Luther a
saint, and the more a saint that he surrendered
his will voluntarily, and was not pinched or
starved or scourged into submission; the more a
saint that he went over to God with banners flying and trumpets blowing, not as a prisoner with
shackled limbs and eyes cast down to the ground.
The moral ideal receives a new coloring at his
hands, but it is not perverted. The standard of
Jesus is thrust up into the sunlight, and flung out
freely to the winds, and carried into the bloody,
dusty fight, but it is the same standard still.

In these modern days of ours, the disposition is
to take the standard down and furl it up and lay
it away. Another order of moral qualities is
coming to honor. If it were the ancient order,
illustrated by Prometheus, Hercules, Perseus, we
need not find fault with it, because these heroes
served humanity after their fashion. The new
standard is the heroic with the heroism left out.
If it were only that for humility we have self reliance; for meekness, self assertion; for patience, impatience; for resignation, restlessness; for submission, revolt; for aspiration, ambition; for disinterestedness, an enlightened selfishness, we could
find cause for partial satisfaction: for self reliance

may be reliance on the nobler selfhood, which is truth, purity, honor; self assertion may be a vindication of fine principles ; impatience may be unwillingness to bear unjust oppression ; restlessness may be discontent with a meaner lot than is decreed ; revolt may be moral protest against iniquitous arrangements ; ambition may be a noble hunger of the mind ; and enlightened selfishness may be a reasonable and kind regard for a general welfare. But unfortunately we are not always allowed to put on the commonly eulogized qualities such generous interpretations. It is the lower self that is uppermost. The individual has his own interest, not that of his fellow creatures, at heart ; the reliance is on smartness, cunning, too often on impudence ; the assertion is insolent; the impatience, passionate ; the restlessness, hot and heedless ; the revolt, unthinking ; the ambition, rude and presumptuous ; the selfishness, not by any means enlightened, but coarse and blind, vulgar and brutal—animal for the most part. The self means the table or the clothes, money, place, power.

The moral ideal of average America is success, and it sanctifies the qualities that secure it. The popular man is the best man, and the best man is the "smart man"—the audacious, the quick witted, the swift and unscrupulous ; the man of ready resources, ingenious methods, bold countenance, the man who can get the ear of the public, and gather people about him. Tweed's popularity excused, in many minds, his robberies. Fisk's magnificence was compensation for his thefts. Success justifies the preacher who so far forgets the Master in himself, that he cannot even tell who the Master was. Success justifies the reformer who makes the reform a stepping-stone to office. Success justifies the politician who says that in politics as in war all is fair. Success justifies in trade, monopoly oppression underselling to ruin a competitor. It is failure that declares against a project, not want of principle. The members of the various "Rings" act on accepted rules of business, and only carry out the rules more audaciously than the ordinary men. The rule is, to get all one can, honestly if possible, but to get all one can. The Evangelical virtues do not rank high in the forum, or on the street. To look out for number one is neither saintly nor heroic. To keep the hand open when there is something to get, and shut when there is something to give, is not following the example of Jesus. To watch your advantage, and make all possible gain from your neighbor, is not strictly according to the Sermon on the Mount.

I cannot quite agree with my excellent friends, that if each one looked out well for himself all would be well looked out for, that consideration for others is a weakness. If we were individuals this would be true. It would be true with the clause that, being individuals, the prosperity of the whole is necessary to the growth of each one. But the popular interpretation defines the creed. It is not as the single philosopher or separate citizen reads it, but as the average man reads it ; and as he reads it, it stands condemned, for he reads it with the eyes of his animal covetousness and greed ; he construes it according to his love of pleasure, or of power, or of notoriety ; he accepts it as a license to make gain howsoever he can from his neighbors, to outshine them, to override them, to enrich himself at their expense, to make them dependent on him, witnesses and servants of his glory. The individualism of the common sort of men in our communities consists in an entire disregard of the rights and claims of others, save in so far as by conceding them he can aggrandize himself. He serves for popularity ; he flatters for praise ; he gives for favor ; he is public spirited when he can obtain by it the public voice ; he is generous when the object has the general sympathy, and when munificence will bring a munificent reward.

In our communities everything·encourages this kind of individualism ; the free opportunity, the open chance, the unlimited competition, the nearness of the prizes, the proximity of the common goal, the demand for activity, the need and the power of money, the accessibility of all places and trusts to him who carries the golden key. It is not strange that in America the moral ideal should be low, that it should become lower and lower under stress of competition and strain of ambition. That the "Evangelical" standard, as it is called, should be completely neglected, put out of sight, put by as an obsolete and useless thing; that the heroic standard should be laughed at and rejected as impracticable, is not surprising. But it is none the less lamentable. For in our communities, too, as in all communities, the bond of humanity is strong. Society in America has to submit to the same eternal laws that regulate society in England and Europe. Americans, like Germans, Frenchmen, Italians, Israelites, are members one of another, and the recognition of this fact is even more vital in a country where the fact, not being presented to us by institutions, forms, and symbols, must be borne in mind by each citizen for himself. Elsewhere the conception of humanity is throned and crowned; here each must enthrone and crown it for himself. In other lands every man must, in some manner, submit, conform, humble himself, keep within limits; if not self-contained, he is contained; containment is a necessity; there are bounds he cannot pass over, rules he must observe, dignities he must respect. Our condition is the nobler—the more privileged, but it is the more responsible and the more dangerous.

Even religion does not help here as it does elsewhere. For not only have we no established church, which stands for unity in the highest plane of humanity, and, secure in its national position, can emphasize with authority the grand virtues and duties of the religious character and life, putting the practical elements foremost, keeping speculative questions in the background, making the individual sensible that he is a member of a grand, consolidated body—ancient, dignified, illustrious, gathering into itself the noblest elements of manly and womanly character. Religion with us is a group of sects, each struggling for existence or preëminence, each profoundly interested in its dogma, each exalting the virtues of loyalty to its cause, and making sectarian fidelity a prime element in the devout character. The sect represents a jagged fragment of humanity, not a rounded whole, however small; and the moral ideal it holds up is anything but beautiful, glorious, or inspiring. Religion with us does not keep in remembrance the simply human facts on which the moral standard rests, but a little mound, a separate heap or pile of facts, on which a sectarian flag may be planted, but on which no edifice can be reared. The consequence is, that qualities quite other than " evangelical " are celebrated as Christian qualities ; sometimes the very reverse of humility, meekness, generosity, sympathy, unselfishness, aspiration, brotherly-kindness. We should be accused of injustice if we said that religion in its coarse popular forms accepts the " smart man " as its model, and counts him best who contributes most to the success of his church.

No individualism or cliqueism has a fine moral ideal. The tall column must have a broad base. The tall tree has wide-spreading roots. No theory of self-culture, self-development, solitary self-perfection results in noble attainment. There must be wholesome and abundant soil. Such theories end in daintiness, superciliousness, exclusiveness, intellectual or æsthetic pride, literary conceit, sentimentalism, moral dilettanteism, moral eccentricity, not infrequently moral turpitude, the end, self-development, being held to justify a cruel disregard of others' feelings, a cruel trifling with others' rights and affections. The bitterest examples of heartlessness have been exhibited by men and women who have set out on this narrow by-path towards individual perfection. Like the boy who shouted " Excelsior," in Longfellow's famous poem, as he climbed the Alpine steep, he perished in the snow. Jesus says, " Be ye perfect, even as your Father in heaven is perfect;"—but in the same breath he declared that the Father in heaven showed himself perfect in showing himself a Father, by identifying himself with his family, by causing his sun to rise on the evil and on the good, and sending rain on the just and on the unjust.

The first touch of genuine humanity awakes from their long slumber the evangelical virtues. We have but to think of our bond of brotherhood with our kind, and once more the fruits of the Spirit are seen to be—love, joy, peace, long-suffering, kindness, goodness, faith, mildness, self-control. Let one consider soberly his place in the nation whereof he is a member, or even in the large community whose life he immediately shares; let him consider the many who are better, wiser, more earnest, more faithful, more useful, than he; let him consider how much more than he can pay he owes, how little of all he possesses he earns, and the result of his consideration must be humility. None are proud save those who never compare themselves with others; and they that might advance the best claim to be proud are the first to disavow it.

Let one consider the comparative effects of violence and gentleness, forgetting if he can, and as he may, his own momentary impulse of anger towards an injurer. Let him fairly take into account the circumstances and conditions; let him estimate the bond of kindness at its full value, and judge calmly of the means by which it may best be preserved unbroken, and he will perceive that meekness is more reasonable as well as more noble than revenge. He will see that "violence is partial and transient, gentleness universal and constant;" that "to bear and to pardon is the wisdom of life."

Let one consider the unavoidable slowness of all progress; the necessary condition of ignorance, stupidity, dullness, in which the mass of mankind still live; the inherited and quite uncontrollable passions; the predominance of appetite over judgment, and of impulse over reason, in all but the very few; the ages long that wisdom and truth and justice have waited for their recognition; and patience will seem to be one of the most self-evident of virtues. Whoso reflects on the long suffering of the divinest attributes will scarcely plume himself on his power to wait his few minutes more or less.

The rule of order in society as among the stars is obedience to the law that arranges, combines, organizes, controls, impels. The planet must not leave its track; the individual must not fall out of the line of providential development. The man's track is harder to find than the planet's; but never in the spirit of revolt, only in the spirit of obedionce can it be found. " Let every soul be subject to the higher powers," said Paul. We say, " Amen," only demanding surety that the powers are higher, and not merely look so, or are stationed so. The higher powers are such as *organize society ;* they are justice, kindness, truth, equity, love. All powers that do not represent these are lower powers, though they be imperial.

Society preaches contentment, for it prescribes the limits within which the man must remain. Society preaches disinterestedness, for it compels us to feel that the wealth of existence is in its sympathy, and sympathy in community of feeling, and community of feeling is impossible unless all share. There is no circle if a link drops out. Society preaches peacefulness for there can be no society without it. Society preaches faith, for its members live by faith—faith in one another, faith in the common end and object, faith in the one law they all obey. Society preaches self control, for that is the power that keeps every wheel in its place. Society preaches joy, for joy is the mainspring of healthfulness, the fountain of refreshment, the electrifying and regenerating spirit. The religion of humanity will restore the Beatitudes to their rank in spiritual regard. It will say once more : " Blessed are the poor in spirit, for their opinions and modest receptiveness will bring them wealth. Blessed are they that mourn, for to them the resources of consoling sympathy will be revealed. Blessed are the meek, for theirs shall be the brotherhood of the gentle, the pure, the saintlike. Blessed are they which do hunger and thirst after righteousness, for they shall be made strong with justice. Blessed are the merciful, for they shall increase and share the blessings of mercy. Blessed are the pure in heart, for about them shall breathe the atmosphere of heaven. Blessed are the peacemakers, for they shall have the joy of helping to make the earth a home. Blessed are they who suffer for their fidelity to the principles of equity and kindness, for in them these principles become potent and kingly; great shall be their reward in the fact that the ruling powers will be more heavenly."

A discerning man has said: " Whatever is worshipped and loved in this world is comprised under two heads—our idea of God and all possible excellence is resolvable into these—Power and Beauty." Religion teaches, the religion of humanity, like every other, that the power to curb demonstration is greater than the power to let it out. The anvil bears up with far mightier force than the hammer bears down, but the hammer has all the motion, and makes all the noise. The Macedonian phalanx—solid, impenetrable, silent, slow-moving, with firm lances and short swords, conquered the hordes of Asia. Wellington's patient lines won Waterloo. It was the force that received the charge, not the force that made it, that gained Gettysburg. Pilate, the representative of the Roman Empire, ordered Jesus to crucifixion, but confessed himself defeated by washing his hands and disavowing responsibility for the innocent blood. The demonstrations of Savonarola and Luther came short of their convictions. They said less than they felt. Their strength was in their power of endurance; the patience with which they waited, the silence in which they meditated, the loneliness with which they prayed, the meekness with which they forbore, the constraint they imposed on themselves, till constraint was no longer possible. The study of any great life reveals the fact that power has been accumulated, gospel-fashion, by patience, obedience, submission, long suffering, the discipline of denial and control. The vapor gathers itself up in clouds before a drop of rain falls; the farmer likes the shower more than the cloud. The demonstration of power is more popular than the power. The qualities of the hero stir the blood. The blast of the trumpet is kindling. The flag, the uniform, the martial step, the dash, the shout, catch the senses and thrill the nerves. Courage, audacity, fearlessness of everything that causes fear—even man and God-defying fearlessness. the temerity of Satan, lays us under a spell that bewitches while it demoralizes. But this is illusion. The fact remains and it will remain, and it will be more and more acknowledged that the passive power takes pre-eminence and precedence of the active. There was no world till the fire-mist was condensed.

And beauty, the moral type of it, will ever hold its own. The room in the Dresden gallery, where stands the Sistine Madonna alone, is always filled with visitors, men and women, from all parts of the world. They sit enchanted before the celestial vision of purity, sweetness, patience, tenderness; the mild glory wherefrom St. Barbara turns her face away for a moment, outshines all the splendors of the royal gallery, all the splendors the visitors possess or dream of, all the gauds they wear. The silence is scarcely disturbed by a whisper, never by a loud voice. The people enter and depart as if the place were a temple; many sit there by the hour, and more than once I saw tears start from the gazing eyes and roll down worn faces, unchecked.

Was the picture so beautiful, and would a loving picture like it be less so? would a character enchant less than a painted canvas? The artists despair of painting a face that should be worthy of Jesus. Art still is faithful to the best tradition, and celebrates in its ideal forms the qualities the world has never ceased to worship

and never learned to imitate. The modern admiration of what are not quite justly called the
" feminine virtues," is a sign that the grace has
not departed, even though the virtues be sometimes miscalled, and very often misinterpreted.
Let art continue to hold high its moral ideal of
beauty. Let religion continue to lay stress on the
qualities it has of old revered. Let humanity be
persuaded that those qualities are its strength.
Build on them what splendid edifices you will ;
add culture, grace, accomplishment, the refinement that charms, the knowledge that enriches,
the aspiration that perfects ; the more beauty the
better, if beauty be made the finishing grace.

IX

IMMORTALITY.

"STRANGE !" said one of our finest thinkers, perhaps our finest, as if in soliloquy—
"strange that the barrel-organ man should ter-
minate every tune with the strain of immortality." The remark calls up a world of thought,
which we have no disposition to analyze. The
suggestion of mechanical fatalism in the phrase
"barrel-organ," as applied to a human being,
coupled with the admission of a steady eternal
prophecy, makes us wish he had said a word
more to explain how a bold spiritual faith could
proceed from a machine. Perhaps the deep mind
was turning the question over, and musingly
dropped a hint of the problem, having no hint
of a solution to offer. This is the problem, the
solution whereof is yet far off. How is it that
mankind always and everywhere, with few and
scattered exceptions, perhaps with no absolute
exceptions—how is it that man as man, the race

of man, dreams of immortality, insists that under one form or another he shall not, cannot die?

For this is the general anticipation. Mankind, it may be broadly asserted, has universally cherished faith in immortality under some form. The form is often crude, fantastic, grotesque; sometimes so uncouth as to be revolting, sometimes so attenuated as to be hardly recognizable, sometimes so eccentric and whimsical as not to merit the name of belief, still, the apprehension is present. A strict definition greatly limits the domain covered by the historical faith; but if we make allowance, as we should, for mental crudeness and grades of undevelopment, the universality of the faith, opinion, guess, anticipation, dream, whatever it be, must be practically conceded. Not that the doctrine of annihilation has never been taught; it has been, but it is at least doubtful if it was ever held in an absolute form. It may be questioned whether the doctrine can be held in an absolute form, whether it is tenable or thinkable. Can the thinking being think of himself as not thinking? Can the sensitive being fancy himself insensible? We can believe in the annihilation of others; can we believe in the annihilation of ourselves? Looking on a lifeless body, it is easy to feel as if all the life that had been associated with it was extinct; indeed it is not easy to feel otherwise. But can one imagine himself to be utterly extinct? Annihilation therefore may be an opinion, but it can hardly be a fixed conviction; it may be a doctrine, but it can hardly be a firm faith. Faith must have something to cling to; it cannot stand fixed in nothing, and annihilation is nothing. Hamlet tries his thought on it:

> " To die:—to sleep,—
> No more : and, by a sleep, to say we end
> The heart ache and the thousand natural shocks
> That flesh is heir to,—'tis a consummation
> Devoutly to be wished. To die,—to sleep,—
> To sleep! perchance to dream ;—ay, there's the rub."

Sleep is not death, though it wears a faint similitude to it, and yet sleep is the only parallel of death we have.

The materialist, while doing his utmost to prove immortality impossible, while affirming that " thought is a motion of matter," that " thought stands in the same relation to the brain as bile to the liver," that "the brain is the sole cause of spirit," that "with the decay and dissolution of its material substratum, the spirit must cease to exist," still preaches the persistency of force, its indestructibility, its continual passage and perpetual transformation. Nothing, he says, dies or can die; modes of existence change and pass, but force endures; at-

oms and powers mock at the mutations of death ;
nothing is lost. Heat may be only a mode of
motion ; feeling, thought, moral purpose, may be
but modes of motion ; the phenomena of conscience, aspiration, will, may be but illusions of
relation and continuation ; but whatever they are,
they are imperishable. Though but ripples on
the surface of a lake, they never cease ; though
but agitations of the atmosphere, the invisible
waves flow on evermore, giving their movement
and never quite subsiding. The consciousness
that holds the mental powers in association for
a time may be loosed, but whatever force there
is, passes undiminished on. Here is a kind of
immortality, an impersonal, unconscious, elemental kind, to be sure, carrying no hearty
cheer, suggesting no individual promise, but it
is something different from utter annihilation,
the exact opposite of that in fact—utter and inexhaustible vitality, the indestructibility of qualities, the perpetual rejuvenescence of powers.
Modern science indeed cannot accept cessation.
It knows no dead matter. It knows no matter
in the ancient sense, and therefore it knows no
death.

Above this class of so-called materialists, for
whom no kind name has been discovered but for
whom that name is inappropriate, are those
who preach an immortality in the race ; preach

it—I use that word designedly, for their teaching has the warmth the earnestness of men who speak under force of moral conviction. This is the doctrine of Comte, after whom the religion of humanity has been mis-named. The individual perishes, as a conscious person; he continues to live in the race as an influence, and the race lives in him. The race is the immortal being, man is immortal, not men. " The social existence of man really consists much more in the continuous succession of generations than in the solidarity of the existing generation," and the successive generations owe their continuance to the onward pressure of the individuals who rise and disappear like successive undulations of the sea. The coral insect bequeaths its tiny wall of limestone to the slowly rising reef. The human frame gains solidity and maturity as it passes through stages of decomposition, its component particles dying that others may succeed to them in the structure. Death carries away the generation that has done its work, and makes room for another whose work is before it. Each is richer than the preceding by all that the preceding has achieved, and will bequeath augmented treasures to that which will come after it. The race is an organization, and the individual men and women are the cells that discharge their momentary function and are then dismissed. The race is not to be compared to an ocean, the component parts whereof are tossing billows or foam-flakes flashing in the sun; it should be likened rather to a forest tree, that assimilates and transmutes the elements that enter into its structure. The idea is simple and intelligible. It has the merit of perfect clearness and of perfect demonstrability. It is true beyond a peradventure.

It is an idea that has exercised considerable influence in history; probably no single idea has possessed a larger amount of vital power. With the Jews the doctrine of immortality in this form had great sway, as well in the older as in the later epochs of the nation. Some have questioned, rashly perhaps, whether any other doctrine than this was entertained by that branch of the Semitic race. The Pharisees certainly had a developed doctrine of personal immortality, and traces of a distinct theory are found before their day. But the personal existence after death was not the most attractive feature of the national hope even with them. The Hebrew apparently knew no hearty existence apart from organization. The disembodied life was hardly worth calling life; the disembodied spirit was a ghost rather than a being. The under world whither the dead repaired was a gloomy abode of shadows, which dimly hovered about, aimless, pointless, with spectral hallucinations, instead of thoughts. Their condition was rather one of supended animation than of life. The smallest possession on this side of the grave was worth more than the greatest on the other side. The Pharisee's hope of resurrection was hope of restoration to his terrestrial existence. His messianic felicity was to be on earth; he was to have his body again, and be with his friends. This was the exclusive privilege of Israel. The followers of Jesus entertained the same expectation. Their master prayed that the kingdom might come on the earth. The millennial reign was looked for as a prolongation under happy auspices of the earthly human estate, with all physical conveniences and delights. The heavenly Jerusalem was solid, with walls of jasper and gates of pearl.

The Hebrew was vital; he believed in things; his prayer was for length of life, and for male children who could perpetuate his line. Death and childlessness he abhorred. Die he must; it was the general doom; but dying, he was consoled in thinking of the children and grandchildren and great-grandchildren who inherited his possessions, his name, his courage and his faith. The book of Deuteronomy puts on record a law that " if brethren live together, and one of them die and have no child, the wife of the dead shall not marry outside to a stranger; her husband's brother shall take her to wife, and the first born whom she beareth shall succeed to the name of his brother which was dead, that his name be not put out of Israel." The losing of his name from Israel was the loss of place in his line, the forfeiture of standing in the nation ; the breaking of the connection between the individual and the great era that was coming. This idea was Jesus confronted with by the Sadducees, who denied the resurrection, but held to the faith of immortality in the race. The book of Ecclesiasticus, by some supposed to be a Sadducean writing, clearly taught this doctrine. " There be that have left a name behind them, that their praises might be reported, and there be that which have no memorial, who are perished as though they had never been, and are become as though they had never been born, and their children after them. The former have been merciful men, whose righteousness has not been forgotten. Their seed standeth fast, and their children for their sakes. Their bodies are buried in peace, but their name liveth for evermore. The people will tell of their wisdom and the congregation will show forth their praise. The inheritance of sinners' children shall perish, and their posterity shall have perpetual reproach." " Have regard to thy name, for that shall continue with thee above a thousand great treasures of gold." " A good life hath but few days ; but a good name endureth forever." The Hebrews found their heaven on earth in a god-fearing and god-favored life.

A belief that animated a race like the Hebrews, so vital, tenacious and energetic, so overcharged with enthusiasm, is not to be spoken of lightly, as if it was the last resort of philosophy driven to desperation. It may be lacking in sentiment, in poetic beauty, refinement, delicacy, but it certainly is not spectral. It is at all events vascular and vigorous. If not spiritual, in the ordinary sense, it is heartily human.

. Are we sure that this belief is not operative now, though not publicly professed or intelligently entertained ? What are they thinking of who toil to perpetuate themselves among men, after they shall be deceased ; who joyless, parsimonious, self-denying, labor to build up and bequeath to their heirs great fortunes that shall after a fashion preserve, keep together, mass, and project far into the future their power of forethought, industry, dominion over things and men, stretching their sceptre, as it were, over realms of future activity when their skeleton hands shall have dropped away into dust ; who put the results of a long, hard, penurious, obscure, unprivileged life into some institution, hospital, orphan-asylum, library, gallery of art, museum, school of design, with which their name shall be connected, through which future generations shall gratefully bear them in mind, and by means of which they shall exert a power of untold and unconjectured extent over many hundreds of their fellow-creatures ; who found families which shall be but the nobler extension of themselves ; make discoveries the utility and reputation whereof shall give them posthumous renown ; write books they hope are destined to live in literature when their authors are no more ; paint pictures, as Turner did, less for money than for future distinction ? A very powerful motive with men is ambition ; but ambition is seldom satisfied without a contemplation of the future. Love of fame is a strong incentive, and love of fame always has reference to an immortality on earth. Fame is impersonal. It is probable that a greater number of strong minds are set working by the hope of such an immortality than by the hope of any personal felicity in another state.

Is it urged that this doctrine may be a good one for the strong and great, but must be very unsatisfactory to the weak and small ? an excellent doctrine for a Newton, a Leibnitz, a Laplace, a Dante, a Milton, a Michael Angelo, or a Rafaelle, but a poor one for Smith and Jones. The objection would be fatal if the immortality in question were an immortality of fame ; but against an immortality of influence it has no force. The multitude of the Smiths and Joneses, the millions of mankind are of more moment to the accumulating life of the race than the few great philosophers, poets, and painters whom men celebrate. There are tens of thousands of families in the United States that never heard of Plato, or Shakespeare, or Columbus, but children are born and reared there, domestic life is kept sweet, constancy is preserved, morals inculcated, religion taught, goodness illustrated, and the force of virtue extended. The sources of power are here. It is the mass of character that determines human condition and decides human destiny. The eminent are not necessarily the useful; the famous are not necessarily the beneficent. Whoever leads a good life, sets a good example, establishes a well-conducted family, rightly orders a home, worthily rears children, honestly pursues a respectable calling, is temperate, frugal, chaste, makes the most precious of contributions to his kind. The great people owe the qualities that distinguish them to little people. The mightiest trees spring from the common ground. New York gets its supply of water not from the queenly Hudson that pours a silver flood from the North to the sea, but from the insignificant Croton, which never floated a ship, whose banks are adorned with no villas, whose praise no poet ever sang.

In humble families the memories of parents and kindred are cherished as devoutly as they are in kings' houses, or in nations' legends. Children live in those that gave them birth, though none but they knew them. The world would be badly off, indeed, did its progress depend on its Platos and Aristotles, its Bacons and Newtons, its Dantes and Shakespeares, its Angelos and Rafaelles. The multitude of mankind never indirectly felt the touch of their influence. The simplest qualities of character are worth to the race more than all art, and poetry, and philosophy. The plain New England farmer, by the help of his prudent wife, rears a family of sons whose virtue is of infinite value to their country in its time of peril. Their work done, they retire from the field, bequeathing their life to their sons, who prove valiant servants in their time. The line runs on for two or three generations, ploughing straight furrows in a crooked world. Of the New England farmer, little or nothing is known; but that he survived his dust, spoke and guided and swayed after he was dead who will deny?

Say what we will, the dead reign over us—not the mighty dead only, whose power is in institutions, literatures, laws, customs, and social ideas, but the forgotten dead, whose blood is in our veins. The dead not only outnumber the living, they outweigh them. The living are the shadows, the dead are the substance. The living make the motions, the dead work the wires. The living are the masks, the dead are the beings. They shape our features, color our skin, eyes, hair. We think their thoughts, enact their wills, continue the exercise of their dominant activities. They fight for us when we are tempted, or they drag us down when we are weak ; they move us to pity, or harden us to hate. We are as puppets in their shadowy hands. They are a destiny ! Some strong-natured ancestor tyrannizes by his vice over generations of his descendants, shooting the arrow of destruction through their vitals, giving them cups of poison to drink which they have made the refusal of impossible. Again, some sweet-souled progenitor acts the part of a guardian angel towards sons and daughters in long succession, who feel the spirit so near that they seem to be in conscious communication with it.

The souls of the dead, though they be unconscious, lurk in our dwellings. All houses wherein men have lived and died, are haunted houses, says the poet. Our frames are haunted houses. The chambers and secret closets of the mind are haunted. We see the spirits, though the spirits do not see us. We feel them, though they are insensible to us. Our lives are in their hands, though their hands are thinner than air.

Yes, this immortality in the race is a very real, a most affecting and impressive thing. It is life of the most vital description; life, the living whereof worthily should be most inspiring; the living whereof unworthily should be terrifying, for it soon passes from our control, and falls into the track of moral law, which is moral predestination.

Is it still urged that this doctrine of immortality is unsatisfactory; that there is no real human immortality, which is not personal; that the only kind of immortality which any one is specially interested in defending, is one in which identity survives death and preserves its consciousness through all changes?

But there is nothing inconsistent with this belief in the doctrine we have been considering. Every argument for personal immortality has all the force it had before. In fact the thought of an organic connection with the race is the thought that more than any other gives dignity to the private hope. The trunk of the oak tree guarantees life to the leaves and twigs. It was faith in the immortal destiny of Israel that emboldened the individual Hebrew to believe in his own. He shared the imperishableness of his root, and felt assured that when Israel was restored, he would be. " As in Adam all die, even so in Christ shall all be made alive," writes Paul the Pharisee : "I am

the vine, ye are the branches." "Because I live,
ye shall live also," says the Logos-Christ of the
fourth gospel. "No man liveth to himself, and no
man dieth to himself," says Paul again, his mind
full of the thought of solidarity. Surely no individual would think of claiming immortality for
himself on private grounds. He has no roots that
reach down through the world. Detach him from
the deep traditions of his kind ; pluck up his stem
from the common earth and set it down in a separate pot of clay, and the thought of his surviving
the winter of death is absurd. Alone in his isolation, sharing no collective life, supported by no
enclosing sympathies, his decease is inevitable.
All his moral qualities imply brotherhood ; his affection, his hope, his aspiration. It is the universal hope, the general desire, the unanimous wish,
the common persuasion of the ages that embol-
dens any one, the wisest and the best, to entertain
the anticipation of rescue from the wreck of matter. The dream that would be wild for me, by
myself, becomes less irrational when cherished
heartily by millions of my race. On the strength
of such multitudinous aspiration I may venture to
aspire.

The assault that has carried outwork after outwork of the popular credence has not yet reached
the citadel of human conviction. The grave of
Lazarus has not been found empty. The resur-

rection body of Jesus has been fading into shadow
of late years, and now is attenuated to an apparition ; the supposition that it may have been even
a spectre is dissolving, and giving place to the notion that it was perhaps an optical illusion, a
fancy, or a wish ; chemistry has reduced the cor-
poreal part to vapor, past resurrection. Philosophy has made havoc among arguments that had
been relied on for hundreds of years. The idea
that the soul is conscious of its own immortality,
the theory that immortality is a natural instinct,
an ineradicable prophecy divinely implanted in
the human mind and guaranteed by the promise
of the eternal, an unquenchable desire, an imperative demand, an inalienable claim that God has
created and on his honor must satisfy,—these opinions have been dissipated by the searching analysis of thought, and they whose belief in immortality rested on them, go disconsolate. But the testimony of the race to the validity of the great hope
is not sensibly shaken by this displacement of arguments and withdrawal of props. The faith au-
thenticates itself, not the bad masonry of its over
rash supporters. It vouches for nothing but the
main current of opinion, and adopts nothing that
does not strike in with that current.

The belief of the Spiritualists is conclusive for
those that hold it. They are undismayed by the
assaults of skepticism on the popular strongholds

of faith ; rather rejoice apparently in their down-fall, having, they are persuaded, something far better, the direct evidence of the senses. They take no interest in the efforts of idealists to ground their conviction on the spiritual phenomena of the mind, being rather disposed to side with those who discredit the fine prophecies of the soul, in the interest of a more stable argument. If spiritualism stands its ground and holds its own, the controversy is at an end. But Spiritualism is still on the defensive so far as the cultivated community is concerned. The decisive battle-field is not found. The victory is not by any general admission won. On each fresh issue the ground is drawn. Both sides confidently anticipate triumph, and neither side obtains it. The hosts of Spiritualism number their tens of thousands, but they do not march under one leader, or swear fealty to the same cause, or shout the same war-cry. They are encamped on different plains. Among them are able and eminent men ; men of great ability and high eminence, weighty in character and name ; but they do not constitute a compact body, nor repeat a uniform creed, nor testify to an identical experience, nor bear with united force on one commanding point, nor agree on how much or how little is demonstrated. Dr. Garth Wilkinson says candidly, " I have long been convinced by the experience of my life as a pioneer in several hetero-

doxies which are rapidly becoming orthodoxies,
that nearly all truth is temperamental to us, or
given in the affections and intuitions, and that discussions and inquiry do little more than feed temperament.... My whole soul, perfectly unconvinci-
ble by the other side, knows this for me, and floods
me with the power of it every hour. Others are
built from the opposite convictions and do vast
material good works in consequence, and can wait
to turn over the next leaf, till they die."*

And so it is. They believe to whom it comes.
The conviction is private and personal, not from
report but from experience. Spiritualism makes
its converts one by one. Its power is not that of
a massive general conviction, possessed of instinctive inherent force, populations and ages
being welded together by it, and by long habit, exercising it and being exercised by it. It is
nothing like the Roman Catholic belief in angels,
a belief stated, formulated, defined, promulgated
by authority, officially interpreted and made the
basis of religious instruction for a thousand years,
till it has come to be almost a belief of humanity.
Before it can obtain a moral power like this over
men, Spiritualism must have been for several
generations the professed belief of great communities ; line after line must have been born into it

---

* Letter to the Committee of the London Dialectical Society. See Report, p. 234.

and reared in it; it must have worked its way into the constitution of the mind, taken secure possession of thought, become one of the necessary faiths, as it were, a faith too familiar to be discussed, too natural to be doubted. If this time ever comes there will be no more investigations, no more committees of inquiry appointed by learned societies, no more labored arguments, no more conversions; the doctrine will simply be taken for granted on the strength of moral assurance, by force of unquestioned tradition. Until this time comes, Spiritualism, however, convincing and satisfactory to those who receive its revelation, cannot command the assent of the uninitiated. Its power as a great human faith is not established. That comes not with mere numbers, but with what we call force of numbers; the compact moral weight of numbers collected, continuous, cumulative, comprehensive, sweeping along with them the masses of mind and character.

Thus far, the only faith that humanity accepts, and has pledged itself to, is the faith in personal persistence after death. The modes of that existence it does not pronounce on, but the existence itself it steadily prophesies through many voices, the commanding voice of priest, prophet, philosopher, the timid but earnest voices of the believing people. The weight of the tradition

bears on this point, and the strength of it consists in the habitual faith mankind have in the
substantial reality and permanency of their intellectual and moral being. This faith remains un-
shaken. The foremost men of science neither affirm nor deny, but simply say they do not know.
They cannot prove, and they cannot disprove ;
their methods are unsuited to such an investigation, and they abandon it ; the future life is beyond their province ; at the extreme limits of
the palpable domain they stand with bended
head ; the spiritual facts their instruments do
not touch. Tyndall says : " The passage from
the physics of the brain to the corresponding
facts of consciousness is unthinkable. Granted
that a definite thought and a definite molecular
action in the brain occur simultaneously, we do
not possess the intellectual organ, nor apparently
any rudiment of an organ which would enable us
to pass by a process of reasoning from one phenomenon to the other. Were our minds and
senses so expanded strengthened and illuminat-
ed as to enable us to see and feel the very molecules of the brain ; were we capable of following all their motions, all their groupings, all
their electrical discharges, if such there be, and
were we intimately acquainted with the corresponding states of thought and feeling, we should
be as far as ever from the solution of the prob-

lem, ' How are these physical processes connected with the facts of consciousness ?' The chasm between the two classes of phenomena would still remain intellectually impassable. Let the consciousness of Love, for example, be associated with a right-handed spiral motion of the molecules of the brain, and the consciousness of Hate with a left-handed spiral motion ; we should then know when we love that the motion is in one direction, and when we hate, that the motion is in the other ; but the why would still remain unanswered."*

This passage expresses the general conviction, more or less intelligent, of mankind. Here faith sits intrenched. From this posture it is not to be driven. Within this stronghold it feels safe. In an unreflecting age the position may look weak ; in an age of immense material activity, it may seem of no real account ; in an age when intellectual power is dissipated on a great diversity of practical enterprises, it may even seem to be abandoned, empty of occupants, deserted by its own defenders ; but every reaction from a period like this brings out the strength of the position with prodigious force. The citadel of a fortified town is quite unnoticed in time of

---

* Tyndall's address to the British Association for the Advancement of Science, on "The Physical Forces and Thought." (Report, XXXVIII., for the year 1868.)

peace. It stands aloof from the places of business and pleasure ; its moat is dry ; the grass covers its casemates and breastworks ; the children play on its harmless ramparts ; the common citizen is scarcely aware of its existence. But let an enemy approach, it swarms with men, the long guns show their teeth, the armory is stocked with weapons, the magazines deliver ammunition, and the town knows where to look for safety. An extreme intellectual subtlety thinks to capture this citadel of faith by ingenious parallels, by deep processes of sapping and mining. M. Hyppolite Taine criticises the statement of Prof. Tyndall in the quotation just made, and by a singularly ingenious analysis tries to bridge over that impassable chasm by showing that the two seemingly different orders of facts are but two different aspects of the same order of facts, " the one single event being known to us in two directly contrary ways."*

The faith of mankind holds itself responsible for no fancies or vagaries, however gravely or piously put forth. M. Taine may be right ; the dart he lets fly at the heart of the mystery may reach its aim. But suppose his conclusion accepted by the small class of thinkers belonging to his school ; until the bulk of mankind join that school ; until men cease to live in their pri-

---

* Taine's " Intelligence," Book IV., Ch. 2.

vate feelings or their social sympathies, in their
affections and hopes ; until they cease to consult
the witness of their moral nature, cease to believe that there is a moral nature, then will they
go on making the same affirmation and uttering
the same prophecies.

Paul's doctrine of the spiritual body—which
was not original with Paul, seeing that it was
current in his nation—the doctrine which was
taken up and elaborated by Swedenborg and is
one of the cardinal doctrines of the New Jerusalem Church, may be unassailable from the scientific side. If there be such a body made of
fine ethereal substance, completely organized in
all its parts, in human form, with eyes ears
brain and features, a spiritual heart beating
in its chest and propelling spiritual blood through
spiritual arteries, spiritual lungs breathing a
spiritual atmosphere*—if there be such a body,
the essential, inmost form using the material
form as a means of manifestation, and laying it
by when it has no more use for it—it must elude
all known methods of search, just as the secret
of life does, or the nature of force. We cannot
prove its existence, but we cannot prove its non-
existence ; and if such a belief had on its side
the weight of a uniform and unanimous tradition,

---

* Giles's " Lectures on the Nature of Spirit, and on Man as
a Spiritual Being."

oriental and occidental, Asiatic, European, Greek, Roman, Teutonic, instead of being, as it is now, the fanciful notion of a small and peculiar sect, it would stand quite unappalled before the threatening advances of science. That it has no such weight of authority in its favor is apparent to all. It is an eccentricity, a little side eddy in the grand movement of the moral tradition, interesting certainly, curious, pleasing to fanciful minds, but standing in no depth of human soil.

The movement of moral tradition confines itself to the tract of moral experience. It is not a speculative movement across a speculative field; it is a moral movement over a moral field. It is a movement of internal experience. It makes small account of special arguments, for or against; it is not checked by local doubts or misgivings, by considerations of private demerit, unworthiness, or insufficiency; it is not turned aside by mental vagaries; it rushes on, bearing skepticism of all kinds away as the Hudson bears away the piles of chip and straw that accumulate at points along its course. Commit yourself fairly to the stream, and your arrival among the islands of the lovely bay is certain.

What can you do with the idealist who plants himself sturdily on the facts of the moral nature, simply stands there, affirming the validity of his spiritual being, and uttering prophecies from the height of his hope? You cannot dislodge him; you cannot refute him; you cannot pretend he is not there. You may launch at him your bold assertion, an equally bold assertion he will launch back at you. You may call him a visionary, he will call you a materialist; you may call him a poet, he will call you a proser; you may call him a dreamer who lives in ecstasy, he will call you a delver who lives in a ditch. He says : " I fall back on my hope. My hope is my argument. It is a note of hand which needs no endorser. My constitution to aspire to endless being is evidence which no miracle can strengthen. Make out hope a part of your nature, no accident or whim, but an angel He despatches, and the case is won. The soul is an immortal principle. It is an indestructible essence. It is part and parcel of the Divinity it adores. It can no more die than he can." " We are conscious of durability as a quality, if not of future duration as a fact." " We ask for evidences of faith. Faith is the evidence." " Spirit is its own proof, which no rarefaction of matter can reach." " If God could make me out of a shell, he can make an angel out of me. If my body be a resurrection from the grave of a trilobite, something finer than enters its own tomb may come out. If clay has mounted into my soul, how high shall my soul mount?" This sounds very much like rhapsody, but it is merely the rhapsodical form of a common-place persuasion. They that live in their affections will not believe that they are perishable. Tennyson cannot feel that his friend is gone. The mother who puts her child in the ground has a persuasion of the organic vitality of the bond that unites them, which no argument will dispel. It may be feeling, but feeling is the larger and stronger part of nature, and it insists on being heard.

Even had keen philosophic thinkers abandoned psychology to the physiologists, and given over the task of maintaining the validity of the facts of the moral consciousness, the cardinal faith would hold; for as that faith was never born of reasoning, so it will considerably outlast reasoning. But philosophy has by no means surrendered its position. Powerful thinkers in France, Germany, England and America, minds well acquainted with the conditions of the question, familiar with scientific achievements and pretensions, contend manfully for the old ground and concede no inch to their adversaries. These men work on the line of tradition in the race. When that tradition shall be exhausted, and an opposite one acquire an equal validity, then the volume of faith which supports individual conviction will strike into new channels and carry minds along to new conclusions ; until then the drift will set towards the eternal sea. To the believers in the doctrine of evolution, faith in personal immortality becomes exceedingly dim and difficult. The notion of soul germs being discarded, and the assumption of a spiritual nature attested by consciousness being dismissed, he is at a loss to find a ground upon which to build a hope. If the human soul or intelligence be but the last term in a process of development that has been going on in the lower orders of creation, an aspiring fountain whose water has been percolating through layers of primeval rock, and is filtered by passing over sand and gravel, he is puzzled to find the peculiar quality that may endow it with immortality, or to conjecture how and when such peculiar quality was imparted. He is deeply troubled that he cannot put his finger on the instant in human delopment when man began to have an independent personality. Is every animal immortal by virtue of the latent intelligence it manifests? If not, at what particular stage of its development does intelligence become possessed of the privilege? Whence the modern man's claims to a destiny unshared by " the men of those developing ages who may have perished like ants that swarm in the pathway of feet ?" The presumption is, that no such claims can be reasonably advanced, that the necessary condition of homogeneousness in the mental quality through all its gradations is fatal to it, that unless a finer analysis of the rational mind shall prove it different in kind and not in degree only from mind partially rational, as in the lower races, or quite irrational and rudimental, as in quadrupeds and birds, the root of immortality is torn up.

Of. course, under the working of the law of evolution, man may develop into a higher creature, but this higher creature will succeed the existing man, as the existing man succeeds the less perfect types of animals. The species will have the benefit of the unfolding, not the individual. Our progeny will be nobler, but we shall be no more than we are. The humanity of a thousand æons hence may walk the golden streets, and tread the floors of topaz and chrysolyte, but we shall be stages in the "altar stairs that slope through darkness up to God." The believer's sole hope of disentanglement, and escape from the coil of creation into individual continuance, lies in the possibility that some seraphic quality may be discovered sitting in the place where the dead body was laid, or flitting away from the inanimate frame, or perchance lurking in the recesses of the living mind.

The doctrine of evolution is not perfected yet, and as to the philosophy of evolution, we are but on the edge of it. The presumptions are threatening, but as yet they are not fatal ; conjecture is not certainty.

The vital conviction of mankind is satisfied with itself thus far. It makes no apologies, and few explanations. Its attempts to account for its own existence are not successful ; its arguments are commonly weak ; its reasonings are so futile that they hardly bear their own weight. You can beat down its guard, and pierce it with deadly wounds, but it will rise with " twenty mortal murders on its crown," and push skepticism from its seat. The more we look into the origin of the belief in conscious immortality, test the supports on which it has been made by its defenders to rest, sift the materials that compose it, scrutinize the characters of the people who entertain it, measure the reach of the anticipation by the minds that cherish it—in a word, sound the reasonableness of the hope, the more we wonder that it should ever have been fostered, that it should ever have taken root. To hold such a belief seems the height of audacity. The visible proofs against it are so numerous and so strong, the improbabilities are antecedently, in the multitude of cases, so overwhelming, and especially in the case of those who hold it most stubbornly, that its mere existence becomes one of the problems of history. The audacity of the belief favors it; its wildness is its guarantee. Were it more reasonable, it would be more questionable. As the race grows older, more experienced, more thoughtful, the faith seems to lose little of its vitality. The problem retains its interest for the best minds and hearts. It takes on different forms, assumes new phases, presents new aspects, seizes on new materials for its sustenance, but still retains the allegiance of men of all conditions, grades of culture, orders of faculty. It is, apparently, still a cardinal faith.

It asks no special defence, and is self-preserving. It gave birth to Spiritualism, not Spiritualism to it; and it does as much to preserve Spiritualism from the perils that gather about it, perils of delusion, imposture, rant, and cant, witlessness and fanaticism, which set thoughtful minds against it, as Spiritualism does to preserve it from the dangers of skepticism and denial. Men are spiritualists, not because their faith in immortality was dead, but because it was alive. As a rule, it would seem the skeptics in regard to immortality denounce Spiritualism as an imposture. It has given origin to the strangest phantasies—witches, fairies, demons, phantoms, and apparitions; but these, in proportion to their strangeness, attest its power.

They are the frantic efforts to grasp what is intangible.

If there be a religion of humanity, a religion that rests its authentication on the basis which humanity furnishes, draws from humanity its inspiration, consults humanity for its principle, adopts, on the whole, the confession that humanity has most persistently made ; if there be a religion of humanity as distinct from a science of humanity, it must make account of such organic beliefs as this, and use them for humanity's welfare. Let science keep them, as far as possible, within the limits of warranted evidence ; let philosophy purge them of superstition—make them sober, chastened, reasonable ; the time is yet far distant when science will overthrow them, or philosophy take the place of them in the human heart. It is the office of religion to keep them alive, to give them the broadest interpretation, to let their sunlight fall fairly upon the fields of the moral being, to make their animating power felt in all motives to effort, improvement, and elevation. The more we feel the power of the universal moral conviction, the more we believe. The more we identify ourselves with that conviction, the more we have assurance. " Great hopes are for great souls," Martineau teaches. " The noble mind believes in destiny, and admits no doom," Bartol declares. Let us add that the greatest souls are great through their humanity, and bequeath their great hopes to it ; that the noble minds are so only as they express humanity ; their nobleness falls back to enrich the common soil from which they grew, and in which every plant and flower of faith has its root.

X.

THE EDUCATION OF CONSCIENCE.

THE title of this chapter foreshadows its idea. If conscience needs educating it is not the thing that divines have given it out to be. It is not an infallible oracle, "an inward judge," "the voice of God in the soul," "the heavenly witness," "the eye of God in the breast," "the unerring loadstone,

> "Which though it trembles and lowly lies,
> Points to the path marked out for us in heaven."

An infallible oracle needs no instructing; the voice of God needs no articulating; the eye of God needs no brightening. The figure of the magnetic needle, which must be isolated and watched, guarded against foreign attractions, the seductions of the neighboring metal, the local currents of electricity that play around the ship, and can be depended on only when kept true to the magnetic meridian, is beautiful and fascinating as poetry, but inconclusive as argument; for the existence of the magnetic meridian is known as a fact; the properties of the magnetic needle have been ascertained by the incessant observations of three hundred years; the flow of the magnetic current has been watched by the keen eyes of science under all conditions, in all parts of the globe. But the existence of the spiritual needle is the very thing in dispute; its meridian has never been marked down, and the currents of tendency it must fall in with in order to be true are as yet untraced. The results of scientific experiment in one of the most carefully examined departments of physics cannot so easily be transferred to the account of the soul. No figures are less trustworthy than figures of speech.

Let us not make light of the majestic unities of conscience. Let us rather hasten at once to emphasize them before another word is said. They roll through history like the tremendous surf-beats on the shore. Pain and pleasure, shame and praise, guilt and innocence, remorse and approval, go hand in hand around the globe. Stand up and shout, be just, truthful, brave, pure, self-denying, beneficent; stand up and say " ought," and you hear the echoes come thundering back from the gleaming summit of the Athenian acropolis, from the seven hills of ancient Rome, from the mountains round about Jerusalem, from the pyramids of Egypt, from the mounds beneath which Nineveh is buried, from the gloomy crags of Sinai, the snowy peaks of the Himalayas; with one voice the tribes of men respond. The sweet-hearted Fenelon says : " The man has not yet been on the earth whô could succeed in establishing over himself or others the maxim that it is nobler to be treacherous than to be sincere ; to be wrathful and vindictive than to be mild and beneficent. The interior and universal master everywhere and always enunciates the same truths." The skeptical Hume responds : " In how many circumstances would an Athenian and a Frenchman of merit certainly resemble each other? Fidelity, truth, justice, courage, temperance, constancy, dignity of mind, these you have omitted, only to insist on the points in which they may by accident differ." We must not forget however that there is another side.

There are moral discords as well as moral harmonies. The needle does not always point to the same star. The conscience of the young man follows impetuously the flood of feeling ; the conscience of the man in middle life points towards the top of ambition, power, success : in old age it points to prudence as the goal of right. The conscience of the misguided lad, O'Connor, bade him waylay and threaten the British Queen ; the conscience of the British public demands that O'Connor be imprisoned and beaten with rods ; the conscience of a certain class of social *savans* reproaches Christendom for wasting so much time in

trying to save the rubbish of humanity ; the conscience of the philanthropist reproaches him if the
smallest fragment of humanity is suffered to perish ; the conscience of the inquisitor commanded
him to burn the stubborn heretic ; the conscience
of the heretic kept him immovable in his stubbornness ; the conscience of Mazzini made him a con-
spirator ; the consciences of the kings and priests
made them hunters of conspiracy ; the conscience of Mr. Garrison constrained him to stir
up war against the slave power ; the conscience of
the Governor of Massachusetts constrained him
to treat Mr. Garrison as a pest of society. In
all these cases conscience is arrayed against
conscience. The eye saw different objects ; the
voice uttered contradictory opinions ; the oracles delivered inconsistent judgments. Against
the Catholic Fenelon we can quote the Catholic Pascal ; and against the skeptic Hume
we may offset the skeptic Montaigne. Pascal
writes : " We see scarcely anything just or unjust that does not change quality in changing
climate. Three degrees of higher latitude over-
turn all jurisprudence. A meridian decides the
truth ; fundamental laws change in a few years ;
right has its epochs. Theft, incest, infanticide, par-
ricide, all have had their place among virtuous
actions. Justice is what is established." And
Montaigne responds : " What sort of truth is that

which mountains limit, which beyond their range
is a lie ?" The theory of the integrity and universality of conscience receives a sore wrenching from
facts and statements like these. They suggest a
doubt whether there be any such faculty as conscience, any such endowment as a moral sense.

Fancy has a fine habit of personifying the operations of mind. Memory makes records on her
tablets ; imagination spreads her wings and soars
away into the empyrean ; contemplation sits in
her watch-tower ; meditation broods in the twilight ; conscience holds solemn assize. " When it
comes night, and the streets are empty, and the
lights are out, and the business and driving and
gaiety are over, and the pall of sleep is drawn
over the senses, and the reason and the will are
no longer on the watch, then conscience comes
out solemnly, and walks about in the silent chambers of the soul, and makes her survey and her
comments ; and sometimes sits down and sternly
reads the records of a life that the waking man
would never look into, and the catalogue of crimes
that are gathering for the judgment. And as
conscience reads and reads aloud and soliloquizes,
you may hear the still, small, deep echo of her
voice, reverberated through the soul's most secret,
unveiled recesses." An impressive pulpit sentence, but a fiction of the fancy, if there ever was
one. Such personification of the mental faculties

is out of date. Conscience is a metaphysical entity, a name. Is what we call " conscience " anything else than the sum of our moral impressions ? And is it not itself the product of education ? Let us take a hint from etymology.

Conscience : conscio, the knowledge of things together, the knowledge of things as related, the knowledge of relations. Conscience and consciousness have the same root, and were once used interchangeably. Thus Milton, in his sonnet :

> " What supports me, dost thou ask?
> The conscience, friend, to have lost them, overplied
> In liberty's defence."

And Hamlet :

> " Thus conscience does make cowards of us all."

Consciousness is perception of the relations between our own thoughts ; conscience is perception of the relations between one's self and others. Consciousness notes internal relations, conscience external. If no common relations are confessed no common rights or duties are admitted, consequently no conscience is felt. The absolute despot has no conscience in regard to his subjects ; the slaveholder has no conscience toward his slaves ; the savage has but a dim crepuscular conscience. Conscience is local and professional.

The trader's conscience holds him answerable for every failure to take advantage of his neighbor in a bargain, and smiles on his fidelity or infidelity to "business principles;" the lawyer's conscience approves of every act done in the interest of his client, and tortures him for every failure to make a point against opposing counsel ; the politician's conscience drags him up to the bar of party exigency and makes loyalty to the candidate the standard of rectitude ; the conscience of the sectarian applauds the falsehood that blackens other creeds, and has no rebuke for the craftiness of the Jesuit, or the scorn of the dogmatist ; his cause is the cause of Christ, and all means that advance that cause are justified. Robert E. Lee obeyed his Virginian conscience, though it bade him violate his soldier's oath ; Robert Anderson obeyed his soldier's conscience, though it bade him abandon his State ; and both died professing their consciences clean. This man's " conscience towards God," does not reproach him in the least for overcrowding his tenement houses, receiving rents from gamblers and prostitutes, " cornering " gold or grain, " watering " stock, or weakening securities. That man's " conscience towards men," gives him full absolution for all his offences against Sabbath proprieties and devout customs.

Conscience reports fidelity to social relations. Before social relations were recognized, conscience could not have existed. All written records testify to its existence, its power, its wide prevalence, its admitted authority, its consent of judgment. But the written record is recent ; man was mature, disciplined, educated, before he committed aught to writing. A papyrus, supposed to be the oldest Scripture extant, translated in one of our popular magazines, " Old and New," implies already an advanced stage of civilization. What æons of experimental morality must have preceded its age ! What myriads of attempts at social adjustment found voice in its sentences ! Are they in unison with other great Scriptures ? They have the same origin. Do the moral results coincide ? The process by which they were arrived at were the same. The identity of the experiences explains the identity of the conclusions.

The sanctions of conscience cluster about three points : the security of life, the security of property, the security of the home. These three things are of universal moment, and of indestructible validity. First of all, life must be safe from open and secret attack ; men must be able to count on their continuance from day to day, to go and come without peril, to reckon confidently on their to-days and to-morrows ; hence mutual understandings, arrangements, compacts, covenants, rules, and principles looking towards that end. It was at a comparatively recent date that men, in the centres of civilization, went unarmed ; the laying aside of weapons proved that men understood each other well enough to dispense with them. In the barbarous period which prevailed in the best society two hundred years ago and prevails now along our own border, it was understood that all attacks should be made in open day, and face to face ; the general conscience condemned the secret foe ; the moral sense was strong enough to guard man against assassination. Now it is strong enough, as a rule, to guard all people against assault. The social sentiment inculcates respect for life, care for its preservation, tender provision for its security, economy in saving even its small fragments. Numerous proverbs express the common feeling. The sentiment pervades even the uninstructed classes. There is forming a solid mass of conviction that will presently render unnecessary all preparation for personal defence.

Next in importance to the security of life, is the security of property. Until one can call what he has his own, can have and hold his earnings, can keep accumulate and use the fruits of his toil, no society is possible ; education in honesty begins with the fact of possession. The thief, after the murderer, is everybody's foe. Efforts to keep him at a distance, to drive him out, to exterminate him began early. In advance of anything like mutual agreement on the subject of mine and thine, they who had something to lose made war on those who had nothing and were presumed to be covetous of their neighbors' goods. The rich man was on his guard against his rich neighbor; the rich men as a class were in league against the poor; poverty was confounded with crime, the distinction between them is not yet generally made; legislation was once emphatically, is even yet decidedly, in the interest of property. In England, not so long ago, the property of the·rich man was held of more account by the state than the life of a poor man. The task of promoting mutual understandings, creating general convictions, establishing universal principles of honest dealing among the different classes of people is very slow and tedious. The discovery that honesty is the best policy is challenged in some quarters theoretically; its practical acceptance is quite limited. A fine conscience of honesty that reckons and discharges all dues, that will adjust on principles of honor the relations between those who have and those who have not, that will give to each his own, to the artisan and the day laborer, the African and the Chinaman, that will place women in the category of persons, and make it morally obligatory to respect every atom of possession—how long will it be before society is educated to that? How long before the average conscience enunciates that?

The third point, domestic peace, the security of family relations, the inviolability of the home, is equally with the other two of universal significance, and the process by which it is attained is from the nature of the case in all generations and among all people precisely the same. The line of discipline is never changed, the character of the experiments is never altered, the result is therefore in every case identical. Social life depends on the security of the family relations. This must be provided for at once. Hence the laws against adultery, fornication, incest, the stigma fixed on domestic infidelity, the guilt associated with the attempt to break up domestic peace ; hence the sanctity attached to the marriage contract, the gradual formation of the sentiment of modesty, chastity, the study given to the problem of the "social evil" and to the causes and remedies for excessive passion; hence the indignation which burns whenever the purity of society is threatened by wild theories or disorderly lives. It is no wonder that the proverbs of all nations are unanimous on this subject, that after so many thousands of years the moral experience should have become a moral nature.

But this moral nature is not coextensive with humanity by any means ; it does not run through society; it lies in strata here and there; it is local in larger or smaller districts. The education of conscience has nowhere reached its height; dishonesty, unveracity, impurity, violence are nowhere abolished completely, are nowhere totally condemned. There are in the best society permissible frauds on servants and strangers, allowable falsehoods which serve as oil to make the social wheels turn smoothly, sanctioned indecencies and harshnesses deemed indispensable to order. The moral sense, in spite of the friction and polishing of centuries, is still in the rough where it should be most refined. In London, Paris, Berlin, New York, Boston, the finely cultured are the few. The more delicate harmonies of conscience are heard by small audiences. No existing community is founded on unveracity, violence and frauds, but no community exists that is quite free from these disorganizing elements. Nowhere is the education of the conscience finished; nowhere has experience produced its perfect result; no state is all through civilized; no society is homogeneous. Society advances slowly after the manner of a grand army between whose vanguard and whose rearguard every description of humanity is included. Foremost go the engineers and surveyors, picked men, alert, sagacious, temperate, patient, tireless, with eyes open, brains busy, nerves steady, will under control, discipline perfect. Next come the leaders, broad in understanding, wise, thoughtful, considerate, firm of purpose, having at heart the interests of all parts of the host. Then follow the solid masses of infantry, under the law of superior will, orderly because trained, each man in his allotted place, the morals of each depending on the steadfastness of the whole. Behind these again, straggle and swarm the crowd of sutlers and scullions, thieves, adventurers, sharpers, beggars, harlots, the scourings of the cities, bohemians, nomads, two-legged wolves and hyenas, representatives of Babylon, Rome, Canaan, of the horrid ages of bitterness and blood, the Arabs, Huns, barbarians of the older world not yet exterminated, people wild, unprincipled, untaught, creatures of lust that live by plunder and have no acquaintance with the rudest elements of the moral law—such as these have no conscience, the mere word has no meaning to their ears.

Had the education of conscience proceeded in accordance with natural laws, had it been an education in actual facts, in actual social relations, had it kept pace with the development of civilization, the voice would be much louder and more commanding than it is. But local schools have taken up the work, fanciful conditions have been substituted for genuine ones, theories of human relations have taken the place of human relations, people have been taught to accommodate themselves to a fantastic world, and the result is what we see. The priests in India declared that every woman who burned herself on the funeral pile of her husband should enjoy his companionship in Paradise for the space of 35,000,000 of years ; the woman who did not thus burn herself, should have no place in Paradise. Hence it became a matter of conscience in India, for women to immolate themselves with the corpses of their husbands, and all efforts on the part of Mohammedan emperors and English governors general to abolish the foolish and unnatural custom, were resisted as assaults on the moral sentiment of the people. The notion was artificial and fantastical, but it educated the conscience of millions of people for several hundred years.

The Romish church taught that error in religion consigned the unbeliever to penal fires, and that, in order to save multitudes from the hideous doom and the disease which entailed it, the heretic should be apprehended, tried, and, if convicted, burned at the stake. Hence it became the conscientious duty of devout Catholics to aid in consigning their unbelieving neighbors to the flames. The fiction was monstrous, but it educated in barbarity the consciences of people whose natural disposition was mild, and made them do deeds which, had they obeyed the instincts of their hearts, they would have abhorred.

In the belief that he should save the natives of Hispaniola from extermination and the heathen Africans from hell, Las Casas, most benevolent of men, initiated the slave trade which is the detestation of the modern moral sense.

The Young Men's Christian Association of New York, persuaded that knowledge is dangerous to orthodoxy, and that science imperils souls, voted that the " Popular Science Monthly " should be excluded from their reading-room. They could not do otherwise ; their theory of the universe forbade. The theory was very absurd ; it had not a scrap of reason in its favor, it was a mere fiction, and a borrowed fiction too ; but it educated the consciences of several hundred admirable young men, who, did they live according to the laws of society, would laugh at it as superstition.

Conscience will not attain to its normal growth till these local and artificial schools are abolished. Even now excellent people justify Abraham in offering his son Isaac as a sacrifice at the bidding of the Lord. They do not perceive that the duty of preserving carefully a lad like that, of nurturing him, teaching him, fitting him for his place at the head of his tribe, the duty imposed by natural affection as well as by a chief's responsibility, was such a bidding of the Lord as nothing on earth or in heaven can gainsay. They do not consider that what the patriarch regarded as a bidding of the Lord was merely a notion, a fancy, a presentiment, a vision of the night, and that the ancient man was really submitting his conscience to the impression of a dream. Consciences cannot thrive on theories; they must have facts, actual facts, working human relations; not the facts of personal feeling, of private emotion or sentiment, not prejudices, traditions, or inward convictions, but solid, tangible, human concerns and interests, that are involved in all human dealings, and are equally dear to all who live in the social world. Such facts are infinite in number and complexity; they are matted thickly together; they compose the substance of all hate and love; their fineness is so extreme as to make them invisible to any but the keenest eyes, and impalpable to any but the most delicate touch; they reach all the way from common utilities to subtle courtesies and amenities; from every-day customs to rarest heroisms and chivalries; from the ordinary dealings of material affairs to the intercourse of friendship and the heavenly sympathies of human beings. The homeliest of them fall in the way of the most careless observer.

the most ethereal of them only seraphic eyes can see.

The deepest moral sayings, maxims, proverbs, precepts are but keen interpretations of these social facts by minds whose swift intuitions report phenomena in advance of the common apprehension. An English naturalist being shown the solitary tooth of an extinct animal, pronounced, amid the derision of his companions, the opinion that it belonged to a ruminating quadruped of great size. The tooth must have been set in a large jaw, the jaw must have belonged to a large head, the neck must have been long and of immense power to sustain so huge a weight, and to sustain the whole in conformity with the laws of organic structure, there must have been at the fore-shoulders a prodigious hump, a pile of muscle. Taking a piece of chalk, he drew on a blackboard a picture of the animal that no man had ever seen. Not long afterwards the skeleton of the creature was dug up in a cave, and in every particular it justified the naturalist's description. How did Mr. Waterhouse Hawkins get at his secret? It was not by guess or conjecture; no angel disclosed it to him; he had no intuition of it implanted in his mind. His trained thought simply ran to and fro along the lines of analogy, and anticipated the necessary action of creative law. Nature justified his unerring scent.

So prophetic minds have discovered afar off the moral principles which were hidden from the men of their generation, and have reported them to the world. When Solomon says: "The robbery of the wicked shall destroy them;" "He that soweth iniquity shall reap vanity;" "He that walketh uprightly walketh surely;"—when Isaiah says: "Woe unto thee that spoilest when thou wast not spoiled, and that dealest treachery when they dealt not treacherously with thee;"—when Paul says: "We know that all things work together for good and them that love God;" "Whatsoever a man soweth that shall he also reap;" they reported the results of the world's moral economy as they came to their intuition. Ordinary eyes did not discover them; it did not appear on the surface that the wicked failed, that the upright were secure in person and possession, that the unjust were caught in their own snare, that all things conspired to help the devout, that the law of compensation cleared up every straw as it went along. To the average mind this is folly; to the superior mind it is necessary truth, simple declaration of fact, announcement of the necessary order of things. The proverb that "Honesty is the best policy" enshrines the belief that honesty is inherent in the constitution of the world, that the creation is organized on that plan, that the working scheme of providence assumes that principle.

It is a magnificent declaration, but we must read
between the lines of history and behind the phenomena of experience to verify it. The surface
facts do not reveal it ; it is not true in the daily
course of events ; people who are destitute of insight must take the saying on faith, and more faith
is required than the multitude possess. " Justice,"
says an old Persian book " is so dear to the Eternal that if at the last day an atom of injustice were
to remain on earth, the universe would shrivel like
a snake-skin to cast it out forever." Where did
the unknown seer learn that deep and awful lesson? Was it the fancy of a visionary mind, a
dream, the wild conjecture of a distempered oriental brain? Was the thought supernaturally imparted or wrought into the original texture of the moral
constitution, hidden from the rest of mankind, obvious only to him ? Was it not rather a swift infer-
ence from what had already transpired in history
of the divine decrees ? a low voice, audible to none
save the most sensitive ear, from the ages of anguish despair and blood, from innumerable battle-
fields, from the vast plains of desolation where imperial cities had once stood, from the grass-cov-
ered mounds that buried kingdoms of iniquity out
sight. The old Persian, as he sate with bowed
head at the end of Time's long whispering-gallery,
caught the last dying confession of the genera-

tions, and breathed that awful sentence into the ear of his own age.

The experience of humanity begets the conscience of humanity. The moral sentiment is not so much the product of inspiration as of transpiration. Moral truth has not been so much communicated to the world, as extracted from the world. This is the guarantee of its permanence, the pledge of its indestructibility. It stands on the everlasting rock of experience ; it has behind it all the past ; it has been tried in the crucible of the ages.

It is said that " the feeling of utility would confine men strictly within the limits of the average utility of any age. Each generation would come to a mutual understanding of the things that would be safe to perform. The instinct of self preservation would be a continual check to the heroism that dies framing its indictment against tyrannies and wrongs. The great men who fling themselves against the scorn and menace of their age could never be born out of general considerations of utility or sympathy. This theory is unable to give any satisfactory explanation of the moral condition of such men as Woolman and John Brown ; of any brakeman or engineer who coolly puts himself to death to save a train ; of Arnold of Winkelried, who gathered in his breast a sheaf of Austrian spears, and felt Swiss liberty trample over him and through the gap." It may be quite true that " the theory that the moral sense was slowly deposited by innumerable successions of selfish experiences " will not account for the deeds of sacrifice that sparkle in the dust of the highway of human progress. Thus crudely stated, the theory will account for nothing but the average low development of mankind, which, by the way, can hardly be accounted for on the theory of innate moral sentiments. This rough statement omits the momentous consideration that the moral experiences of mankind in the mass are but the clumsy wholesale attempts to arrive at the perfect comprehension of social laws, and makes no allowance for the power of remarkable minds to see further than their contemporaries, or for the power of highly gifted natures to act on quite other than vulgar principles. What right have we to limit the scope of any great law? The witty essayist says: " Sympathy that was spawned by the physical circumstances of remote ages could never reach the temper of consideration for the few against the custom of the many. You could no more extract heroism from such a beginning of the moral sense than sunbeams from cucumbers." But does not the human embryo pass through all the lower stages of development on the way to his own? Has not his organization been worked out from quadruped, fish and reptile? Is not the human brain of Shakespeare and Goethe the last result of innumerable experiments on nervous structure from the crawling worm and the flying bird onwards? Can we explain why the soil of a small territory on the Rhine valley produces the Johannisberg grape? The duke of Argyll thought he had found a fatal objection to the law of natural selection in the splendid decorations of birds. "Mere ornament and variety of form," he says, "and these for their own sake, is the only principle or rule with reference to which creative power seems to have worked. A crest of topaz is no better in the struggle for existence than a crest of sapphire. A frill ending in spangles of the emerald is no better in the battle of life than a frill ending in spangles of ruby. A tail is not affected for the purposes of flight whether its marginal or its central feathers are decorated with white." Yet observation and experiment have shown that the duke of Argyll is mistaken, that the law of natural selection does run out into these exquisite applications, that the humming-birds do put on their gorgeous panoply of azure and emerald that they may come out conquerors in the battle of life. Mr. Darwin has even proved that flowers deck themselves more gloriously than Solomon and perfume themselves more deliciously than Thebe's queen, that they may the more successfully engage in the struggle for existence. If the law of self-preservation will

give to the butterfly its brilliancy and to the lily
its whiteness, why should not the same law, working
out the safety and felicity of man, bestow the daz-
zling qualities of the hero the sweet fragrance of
the philanthropist and the transparent purity of
the saint?

Let the effort at complete adjustment of social relations be sincere and constant, and the
education of conscience will be as even as it
will be rational. The natural method is the
beautiful method. It is false education that makes
the false conscience, partial education that makes
the partial conscience. The narrow conscience
of the sectarian, the unscrupulous conscience of
the trader, the furious conscience of the fanatic,
the technical conscience of the advocate, the
accommodating conscience of the politician, the
austere conscience of the magistrate, the timid
conscience of the conservative, the official conscience of the churchman, is the product of
an artificial school. A return to nature would
correct all this tendency to vagary, which en-
dangers safety perverts equity poisons honor
makes truth impossible and tears kindness in
pieces. Come back to the obvious facts of nature that lie in the path we tread in. Let each
be faithful to his relations such as they are.
Let each keep firm and polished the links in
his short chain. He that is faithful in that

which is least, is faithful also in much. The law of gravitation is the same for the rain drop, as for the solar system. The rules of trigonometry are the same for measuring the distance of the moon as for measuring the height of a tower on a hill-top. He that has a perfectly sound conscience towards a single human being, has a perfectly sound conscience towards all human beings; he that has a conscience void of offence towards his neighbor, may be sure there is no break in the chain that connects him with the eternal law.

XI.

THE SOUL OF GOOD IN EVIL.

AT the close of the Bible description of creation, it is said that God looked on all that he had made, and pronounced it very good :—a recognition this, that the soul of things was Goodness. Till experience had startled men into self-consciousness, and observation had shown them the moral ugliness of the world they lived in, this simple faith remained undisturbed. The notion of a Fall must have occurred to them at a comparatively late period, long after their personal and social Eden had been broken up, and the accompanying idea of Satan was an admission that the innocent faith of the children of humanity had gone. When the stage of history was narrow, and the scenes of existence were few, and social life was simple, and human interests were grouped together in limited communities and on a petty scale ; when there was no geography or history, and the least possible intercourse between States, evil may well have seemed a manageable thing, an instrument in the hands of God for the discipline of his children, owing its character to the will that used it. Thus it was regarded by the early Hebrews. Jehovah employed evil as his scourge, made himself wholly responsible for it, assumed its paternity. In the most ingenuous way the Lord God is spoken of as causing noisome beasts to pass through the land and make it desolate, as bringing a sword into the land and pouring out his fury on it in blood, or sending a pestilence into it. He putteth out the candle of the wicked; he distributeth sorrows in his anger; he hardens the heart of those he would destroy; he seals with the spirit of deep sleep the eyes of prophets rulers and seers; he causes the prophets to prophesy falsely, and dreamers to dream vain dreams, that he may test the people's faith in him. Sickness, calamity and death are his ministers. Is there evil in the city, He cries, that the Lord hath not done?

But this child-like view of the matter could not last long. Knowledge comes with observation experience and reflection; there is some apprehension of the width and complexity of the human world; moral phenomena increase in number and weight; questions multiply; difficulties accumulate; the simple explanations of

the provincial break down ; evil becomes too
massive a thing to be handled by the feeble
wits of villagers ; it drops away from the grasp
of the Lord of Israel, and becomes to thought,
a separate world with a ruler of its own,—Satan. " Lo this I have found," says one of the
later of the Old Testament books, " that God
made men upright, but that they devised many
witty inventions ;" and a later book still, " The
Wisdom of Solomon," says " God created all
things that they might have their being, and
the generations of the world were healthful, and
there was no poison of destruction in them,
nor any kingdom of death on the earth. But
ungodly men called it upon them by their works
and words." " God created man to be immortal ; but through envy of the devil, death came
into the world, and they that hold on his side
find it."

From this time on, evil has been regarded as
a power, a dominion presided over by a dæmon-
ic force, malignant in its disposition, cruel in
its methods, hateful in its ends and processes ;
an enemy of God and men, engaged ceaselessly
in efforts to thwart, baffle, and bring to naught
the designs of the beneficent Father of Mankind. There were those hopeful enough to believe that the benignant power would come out
victorious at last ; some even dared to trust

that the devil would be converted; many accepted on faith the assurance that the works
of the malignant power might be overruled for
the benefit of the faithful, who clung to the
merits of Christ and had confidence in the victorious efficacy of the cross. But that evil itself was anything but what it seemed to be, a
dark, cruel, inimical thing, a spot, a poison
drop, a deadly element in the economy of the
universe, few ventured to believe, at least within the circumference of Christendom.

The modern world has received a better faith;
from what quarter it is not easy to tell, from
many quarters probably—from the purer religious
sentiment which is always soaring above the
clouds and revelling in the deep blue of the inner skies; from the spiritual worship which will
have none but a spiritual, that is a serene,
transcendent deity; from the higher philosophy,
which can not brook the conception of a divided discordant universe; from observation,
which shows evil to be evanescent; from reflection, which gives assurance that it must be
so; from science, which discloses unity, and
sympathy between all orders of phenomena;
from fresh energy, progress, achievement, which,
pushing steadily against all the forms of evil,
finds them movable and removable; from the
spirit of reform, which delights in the discov-

ery that the world can be fashioned anew, and which gains stimulus and courage from the resistance it encounters, sharpening its battle blade against the steel that opposes it. It was Shakespeare who struck out the happy phrase that gathers up in a fine sentence all this new faith and feeling, condensing into half a dozen words, as was his wont, a whole system of philosophy. King Henry ·V., on the eve of Agincourt, enters with two of his lords, like him anxious about the issue of the next day's fight. The king's spirit is greater than his fortune. The desperate condition of his forces he sees.

> " Gloster, tis true that we are in great danger,
> The greater therefore should our courage be.
> Good morrow, brother Bedford !   God almighty !
> There is some soul of goodness in things evil,
> Would men observingly distill it out ;
> For our bad neighbor makes us early stirrers,
> Which is both healthful and good husbandry :
> Besides they are our outward consciences
> And preachers to us all, admonishing
> That we should dress us fairly for our end.
> Thus may we gather honey from the weed
> And make a moral of the Devil himself."

Again, in another play, the exiled duke in the forest of Arden, exclaims :

> " Hath not old custom made this life more sweet
> Than that of painted pomp ? Are not these woods
> More free from peril than the envious court?

Here feel we but the penalty of Adam, —
The season's difference—as, the icy fang
And churlish chiding of the Winter's wind.
Sweet are the uses of adversity
Which, like the toad, ugly and venomous,
Wears yet a precious jewel in his head ;
And this our life, exempt from public haunt,
Finds tongues in trees, books in the running brooks,
Sermons in stones, and good in everything."

A sweet expression of the faith that good comes out of evil ; and if good comes out of evil, good must be in it, the water in its desert, the fountain in its rock. If evil ministers to good, if good is the upshot and issue of it, then good is the soul of it ; the tendency and intent of it is good. It is part of the ministry of Providence, a feature in the divine arrangement of things. Shakespeare but voices the instinctive faith of mankind in regard to physical evils. Hunger, thirst, cold, exposure, hardship, peril, are, he says, the ministers of manhood. Personal evil most assuredly is. Sickness puts us on the study of health ; pain compels us to discover reliefs and ameliorations ; fracture and decay instruct us in the arts of reparation ; courage is born of suffering and deprivation. A brave young man on the very edge of his career meets with the misfortune of the utter loss of an eye, through an accident. The loss seemed an irreparable calamity. The youth was passionately devoted to a pursuit which demanded perpetual use of strong eyesight, and it was feared not merely that a noble face would be disfigured, but that a useful career would be cut short. But he will not so look on his calamity. It has even, he declares, been a gain to him. It has not impeded seriously the pursuit of his profession, and it has turned towards him a degree of interest he could not otherwise have claimed or hoped for, while it has deepened within him the qualities of courage and faith, which are more precious than any outward good.

The graver evils that men dread and shun testify to the same truth that evil contains an elixir that is meant for healing. No evil is more universally regarded as such than poverty. It is the evil all men dread in proportion as they understand it. To multitudes it is the sum of all evils : it is hunger, nakedness, cold, squalor, obscurity, deprivation, loneliness, weakness, sickness, joylessness, lack of pleasure, want of opportunity, failure of development, closing of the gates of advantage. But the only school in which men learn to escape and overcome poverty is poverty. It is the pain of poverty that drives men as by whip and spur to the far-off difficult fields where wealth is. Civilization is the child of poverty. All useful arts, comforts, luxuries, are born of poverty. London and New York draw sustenance from this exhaust-less breast. If poverty, in some relative shape, should cease, modern society would languish for want of motive. It is the fear of poverty, the de-sire to get out of it, the passion to leave it behind, the terror of falling back into it or into some de-gree of it, that scourges on the flagging energies of mankind, multiplies their inventions, quickens their faculties. The poor, it is said, are all who labor. How long would any labor if they ceased to desire more than they have?

Conflagration is an evil, but the burned city rises from its ashes in new beauty. Famine is a dire evil, but it teaches scientific agriculture, rota-tion of crops, the economy of the soil. Pestilence is an evil of hideous proportions, but without it the resources of hygiene would remain undevel-oped, and the laws of health would be unknown and unapplied. Disease is an evil, but the bene-ficent science of medicine owes its mature accom-plishments to it. Each form of agony creates its cure; each tortured nerve starts a healing instru-ment into existence. Bad government is an evil of vast magnitude and bitter effect, but the inesti-mable blessings of good government are due to the efforts of trampled humanity to extricate itself from the nets which despotism weaves and spreads. Crime is an evil, but without its unwilling aid laws would never approximate to justice. Vice is an evil, but virtue takes occasion from it to show its colors and train its powers. This is trite wisdom, but trite wisdom is demonstrated wisdom ; wisdom made sound and smooth by attrition, and there is no harm in giving it a higher polish by more attrition.

The Son of Man, we are told, was perfected through suffering. The Son of Man, that is humanity, not each individual ; each individual is not, though many individuals are ; but the race, the Son of Man is. And this suffices to establish the rule ; this demonstrates the general purpose ; this indicates the universal law. It is the rule that seeds put into the ground shall fructify ; millions do not, but the harvest on a thousand fields makes us oblivious of their destruction. It is the rule that children who are born of sound parents shall live ; thousands do not, but the augmenting populations pass silently by the Rachels weeping for their lost ones, and march majestically past the graves where the untimely dead are sleeping. The general experience attests the general principle, and the general principle vouches for the universal principle. The soul of good may not be discernible in everything that befalls, but it is plainly discoverable in the broad facts of evil.

In what has been said thus far we have but touched on the familiar doctrine that evil is a minister to good, that good may be extracted from it by faith and patience and valor; that good holds evil in its grasp and forces healing juices from it by pressure. But we are justified in pushing our investigation a step further. We are justified in maintaining not merely that evil is overruled by good, that good may be extracted from it, that good is in it as a hidden elixir, but that good is the beginning of it, the originator and maker of it, its *causing* soul.

The symbol of evil is the venomous serpent, with glittering eye and shining crest and jewelled skin sliding insidiously through the grass, graceful, beautiful, deadly. Is it not a confession that men saw in evil a soul of good, that they took the serpent as their symbol of wisdom, of life, of eternity, that they even accepted it as the emblem of salvation? the deceiver one with the Saviour? The naturalist tells us that through that form as through all other unsightly repulsive forms of snake, saurian, monster, the creative thought pushes its way onward to its noblest organizations. The snake is a glittering bridge across a chasm. The creator does not leap from point to point in his royal passage from chaos to cosmos. He slides, creeps, flies, rides on the beetle, swims with the fish, skims the air with the bird, tramps thunderingly on with the elephant, ranges with the lion and the tiger, avails himself of chips and straws for boats, and whatever form he makes or uses becomes at once sanctified by the touch of his hand or foot.

The ugly reptile is sacred and beautiful because he has aided the Almighty in his progress towards perfection. The divine purpose found him indispensable. He is in his place as servant of the supreme beneficence. He passes the soul of goodness on. The primal love it was that called the creature into being, and fitted him into his proper nook. And in the chain of gold every link is golden. Even the snake is a gliding, inarticulate whisper of the wood. The mystic name shines in hieroglyph on his glittering scales. The part the serpent is fabled to have played in the Garden of Eden associates him at once with the supreme creative purpose that comprehended centuries and a world. He is the tempter, but he tempts to wisdom and insight into the secret of life. The serpent said unto the woman : " Ye shall surely not die, for God doth know that in the day ye eat of the fruit of the tree, your eyes shall be opened, and ye shall be as gods, knowing good and evil." The serpent suggested the promise of fortune, science, art, culture, civilization ; he was the instrument of progress in material and moral things. The woman listened to him and persuaded her husband to eat. They ate and the promise was kept. Their eyes were opened. Eden was forfeited, but the heavenly Jerusalem was built. The first sin was the first triumph of virtue. The fall was the first step forward. The advent of evil was the dawn of in-

telligence, discernment, enterprise, aspiration.
Eden was the scene of humanity's birth, The
tempter was Lucifer — the bringer of light.
Thus even in him is something prophetic of salvation. The fault of Adam was disobedience to spoken law; but disobedience to arbitrary spoken decree, to unreasoning command, what is that but in
essence obedience to the unspoken command of
intelligence, and what is that but the soul of goodness?

Theodore Parker said this startling thing
about crime: that the increase of crime marked
the progress of humanity. What he meant was
not that all crime was beneficent, that crime
was not an evil, that criminals as a class were
benefactors of society, that every time men
broke through law they broke a prison and issued into worthier life; that the petty thief, the
bold robber, the midnight house-breaker, and
assassin laid society under a debt of gratitude. Such doctrine would make law an evil.
He meant that the resistance to temporary and
arbitrary enactments revealed the power to which
men owed their deliverance from personal thrall-
doms. All breaking of law, even the noblest,
is crime, and he was thinking of that noblest
infraction which emancipates intelligence and
gives scope to justice, the passionate rebellion
of animal desire against moral restraint being

for the moment forgotten. He had in mind such criminals as Cromwell, and Washington, and the host of social and religious reformers who have burst the gates of brass and rent the bars of iron in sunder, and who in their time were pronounced criminals by the authorities that would have fettered mankind. The spirit that actuated such as these was the spirit of faith, courage, hope, aspiration, the regenerating spirit in all time. The minor criminals who break the laws that curb their grossness and would constrain them to goodness are left out of the account in considering the grand movement by which law is purified and authority widened and equity enlarged. There is even in these, perhaps, less of the soul of evil than we commonly imagine ; they do not always mean as dangerously as they behave, and often they act under the pressure of motives which though mistaken are not malignant. I dare not say that in the lower criminal classes, a discerning eye may not discover at last traces of a soul of good, strangely misshapen and distorted, darkened by want of instruction, perverted by cross currents of wild passion, but still to its own apprehension appreciable and justifiable. They too may be, sometimes as we know are, actuated by feelings of resentment not against any laws they ought to obey, but against enact-

ments and arrangements that seem iniquitous.
They look on themselves as emancipators after
their fashion, not in the grand way of Cromwell and Washington, the way that leads to
immortality, but in an humbler way that leads
at best to a little more comfort, better bread for
their hunger—a tighter roof to protect them
from the storm.

Among the gross evils that stand out in dis-
gusting prominence in the record of social experience, there are few that may not be traced
back to a sound, sweet root of goodness. The
evil of self-immolation occurs to us, wide-spread,
hideous, oppressive. Much of it has disappeared
from our view forever. We do not see the
Yogi crawling painfully across the country, sitting in agonizing postures in the very eye of
the sun, or swinging himself over blazing fires;
we know nothing of devotees cutting themselves
with knives, or pillar saints sitting on the top
of columns, or flagellants scourging themselves
along the streets, or ascetics fasting till the flesh
is all wasted from their bones. What we do
see is men and women emaciating their minds
within their bodies, perching themselves high
up on dogmas that lift them in intellectual
squalor above the communion of their fellow
men, whipping their souls with unnecessary
doubts and fears, starving their affections, and

crawling through life in abject misery. The phenomenon is the same in all parts of the world, and the thing expressed by it is the same. And what is the thing expressed? Is it not this, that men will undergo any torture for that which to them is sacred? Through these pains and penances they seek peace. They are in love with something that to them is infinitely more precious than bodily ease, a pleasure of life, private distinction, fame, power, social eminence, or even culture and growth of their mental faculties. They are crying for what they think light; they are creeping towards the kingdom they have dreamed of; they are pinching themselves the better to pass through the strait and narrow way that leads to life. The soul of goodness in this dreary fact of physical and mental disfigurement, is *aspiration after bliss*, a soul the dignity and sweetness whereof should be the more evident, the more ghastly its struggles into expression.

Through much of man's cruel treatment of his brother the same soul shines. It irradiates the shocking ceremonies of human sacrifice. The victim chosen for immolation, led in solemn procession to the altar, laid thereon with holiest rites and slain with the consecrated knife, was the purest, the sweetest, the fittest for heaven and the nearest to it already. The rite was one of dismissal of the holiest to the holiest seats. The victim was regarded as a privileged person, his selection an honor, his fate a blessing. He was sent up as a messenger to the pure gods who were supposed to be ready to receive one so nearly akin to themselves. He was the best gift humanity had to offer ; their tenderest expression of affection ; their living human prayer. It was thus they touched godhead with their humanity, lifting it into the light of the happy ones, lodging it as it were with their own hands in its predestined home.

An interpretation equally generous and equally just may in the same spirit be put on that other frightful fact of history, religious persecution. That is a dismal story of wrong, sorrow and cruelty, a story of evil under almost every form, a story of poverty, exile, bloodshed, of ruined interest, desolated homes, ravaged fields, burned cities, slaughtered multitudes. The worst of it has been told, and will never be repeated, but the end of it has never been reached yet, nor will it be for many a hundred years. Religious persecution is still an evil of no small magnitude, an evil temporal, social and spiritual, touching nearly the most sensitive relations of mankind. Yet the soul of this evil too was Faith. In no period have the persecutors been deeply at heart haters of their kind. Some whose zeal was most consuming, whose record was the reddest, were earnest noble, God-fearing, oven kindly men. Philip II., the most ferocious of them all, would have abhorred himself could he in his breast have detected a single spark of pure inhumanity. They were simply enthusiasts and fanatics of faith, grim and desperate lovers of souls. Their wrath was the "wrath of the lamb." One idea possessed them all, that to have the right faith, to be of the Lord's own, to get admittance into the celestial kingdom, to enter into life, was worth more than all things else, was a boon cheaply purchased at the cost of money, comfort, home, country, life itself. And to this was added another idea, that they who possessed this privilege were bound by duty to their own souls to bring others into it by all the means at their command.

With the soundness of their reasoning I have at present no concern. Its results are its best refutation. What I wish to note now is the hidden motive that impelled them, and to lift it out of the rank of motives that degrade into the rank of motives that dignify and exalt. The body of persecution was and still is loathsome to contemplate. But the soul of it was pure. Say, if you will, that the faith itself was a misfortune, that had men believed less intensely, had they cherished a less intense "love of souls," the world would have been spared vast accumulations of woe, that the "love of souls" was a deplorable disease, that such zeal for the Lord was a madness, and therefore evil was the soul of evil; I reply that the consequence cannot in this way condemn the cause. A sparkling spring may undermine a dwelling; a fresh mountain torrent may overflow a valley; as the ruin does not condemn the rivulet, as the .rotted harvest does not reflect on the mountain torrent, neither does the ravage of the sword and flame pollute the sweet fount of aspiration which, misled through mischievous channels, have spread desolation through society.

The discussions about slavery previous to the last decade, disclosed the fact that this institution owed its origin, in part at least and in no inconsiderable degree, to causes rather honorable than otherwise to human nature, to a disposition to save life, to economize labor, and to add to the cumulative force of social power in the great families that were the centres of growing communities. The slave was made an integral part of the household, was incorporated in fact into the strong living organization which alone in primitive times represented civility and law. The slave was included in the family. "The tie which bound him to his master was regarded as one of the same general character with that which united every other member of the group to his chieftain." It was a rude effort at organizing labor, at consolidating society. There is clear evidence that to be reduced to slavery was, in ancient times, considered a privilege; it meant mercy, protection, care, an introduction into a calmer lot, a guarantee of human rights, a dim recognition of responsibility and worth.* Every instructed American knows that religious zeal had more to do than greed or contempt with the introduction of the negro to this continent. He was brought hither in Christian pity to see the mysteries of the kingdom; mysteries indeed he found them, mysteries of another kingdom whose ruler was the Prince of Darkness. But it was not the Prince of Darkness that opened to him the gates of the new world. It was the Prince of Peace who brought him to the threshold, but could not keep him under the protection of his hand.

Of the evils that weigh heavily on our society, none, confessedly, is more grave than the comprehensive and bitter disability of woman. It is felt in all classes, in every department, and in nearly all relations. It is national, social, domestic, personal. It is felt in the paralysis of the person and in the crippling of the lot. It is felt negatively, in the loss of opportunity, and positively in the obstruction of energy. Woman groans under it; man suffers from it, all the more terribly if he does not groan. To depict the nature of the evil is unnecessary here, for it is known to all. It is

---

* (See Deuteronomy xx., 10, etc., Maine's " Ancient Law," p. 156–8.)

unnecessary to describe its extent, for that too is
no secret to those who care to see. I have no disposition to exaggerate either, nor am I in the
smallest degree inclined to underrate either. A
great writer * says: "The wife in England is the
actual bondservant of her husband. She vows a
life-long obedience to him at the altar, and is held to
it all through her life by law." "She can acquire
no property but for him; the instant it becomes
hers, even if by inheritance, it becomes *ipso facto*
his." "No slave is a slave to the same lengths,
and in so full a sense of the word, as a wife is."
"However brutal a tyrant she may unfortunately
be chained to, he can claim from her and enforce
the lowest degradation of a human being." "This
is her legal state, and from this state she has no
means of withdrawing herself." That is a fearful
picture, and is a just one taking the legislator for
artist. Custom, no doubt, softens it in many of its
features. American custom, probably, softens it
more than English. But suppose in its darkest
colors it be accepted. Suppose all to be true that
the most zealous champions of woman's rights and
the most impassioned delineators of her wrongs
allege; must we therefore jump at the conclusion
that this huge accumulation of misery and iniquity
had its primal origin in violence and fraud? Must
we say, with the great writer just quoted, that
"the inequality of rights between men and women

* (J. S. Mill, "Subjection of Women," p. 54–55.

has no other source than the law of the strongest ?"
that "in the case of women, each individual of
the subject class is in a chronic state of bribery
and intimidation combined ?" that "all men, except the most brutal, desire to have, in the woman
most nearly connected with them, not a forced
slave, but a willing one, not a slave merely but a
favorite?" and that "therefore they have put
everything in practice to enslave their minds?"
Must we agree that "the great mass of influence
over the minds of women having been acquired,
an instinct of selfishness made men avail themselves of it to the utmost as a means of holding
women in subjection ?"

The deepest students into this melancholy history bring back a more cheerful report of their
discoveries. They assure us that the real root of
all this bitterness was not bitter ; that the tyranny
complained of was the tyranny of a crude, rough,
unintelligent but still well-meaning kindness.
They tell us that "the relation of a female to the
family in which she was born, was much stricter,
closer and more durable than that which united
her male kinsman," the woman in rude times of
strife and pillage and lust, "having no capacity to
become the head of a new family, and the root of
a new set of parental powers." In an age when
guardianship was needed, hers was a condition of
perpetual guardianship, necessary to preserve her
purity and to secure for her a social position.

Her family were her protectors; her family became responsible for her. Her father's authority was her shield, his power her defence, his wealth her provision. Insult to her was affront to him; wrong to her brought down his vengeance. She was rooted in the family, could not detach herself, could not be detached, for in passing from the guardianship of parents she passed into the guardianship of a second parent. *Her husband was in law her father.** It was in his capacity of father that he acquired rights over her person and property. She was not his slave, but his daughter, his own blood as it were, part and parcel of himself. The worst injustices, the worst indignities against women, had this kindly root. Polygamy was in its origin a gracious provision against helplessness; whole centuries lie between the evil and its origin; the root of it is so deep under the ground that none but the keenest sighted naturalists suspect it. But if it is there, its existence proves that whatever reforms may be needed now, no reproach can be cast on the original feeling from which the present iniquities have sprung. It is only indirectly and in a secondary way that they reflect on the primitive impulses of human nature; it is only remotely that they bring into disrepute the laws that control the progress of the world. If in things most evil there is a *soul* of goodness, our faith in the moral constitution of things is justi-

* Maine's "Ancient Law," p. 147–149.

fied. The most astounding problems cease to be
appalling. We can feel that mankind have been
groping after improvement; that they have done
what was in them as they saw and knew; that
they sought the true and good, as they understood
them, and through the only means within their
reach. We feel that our duty consists in carrying
out the original intention, not in thwarting it, in
strengthening the creative principle, not in erad-
icating it.

That the soul of goodness is in every case hidden might be expected. Certainly it is; all roots
are hidden; the root of evil more deeply than
any. In some cases it is so well concealed as
to be thus far undiscoverable. But faith assures
us that it will be discovered in due time. Though
of the soul of things little is known, enough is
known to create a buoyant confidence in the
sweetening, saving powers of society; a confidence
that breaks out in the familiar expressions, "It is
all for the best;" "It will all come out right in
the end;" "Ever the right comes uppermost."
That confidence has its root in a faith which rests
serenely on the constitution of human nature, and
assumes a principle of perpetual renovation working at the core of things; a faith that stills the
troubled sea of existence and causes doubt, fear,
sorrow and the agony of disbelief to " vanish like
evanescent waves in the deeps of eternity and the
immensity of God."

XII.

THE SOUL OF TRUTH IN ERROR.

IN the New Testament the spirit of evil and the spirit of falsehood are one. Satan is the father of lies. Jesus says to the unbelieving Jews : " Ye are of your father the devil ; he was a murderer from the beginning, and abode not in the truth, because there is no truth in him. When he speaketh a lie, he speaketh of his own, for he is a liar, and the father of it." Paul speaks of the " working of Satan with all power and signs and lying wonders, and with all unrighteous deceit." " Who is a liar," asks John, " but he that denieth that Jesus is the Christ? He that denieth the Father and the Son is Antichrist." " Many deceivers are come into the world, who confess not that Jesus Christ is come in the flesh. This is a deceiver and an antichrist." And again in Revelations : " And he laid hold on the dragon, that old serpent, which is the devil, and cast him into the bottomless pit, and shut him up, and set a seal upon him, that he should *deceive* the nations no more." These early believers, in the simplicity of their faith, cannot persuade themselves that one who differs from them in opinion can be sincere. They who are not disciples are knaves. They who teach other doctrines are impostors. Heresy and falsehood are synonymous terms. As their own belief became clear and firm, a feeling of infallibility accompanied it. The disciples wanted to call down fire from heaven on the Samaritans who rejected the Master. They were of another party, therefore they were of the devil. This sense of certainty, this utter confidence of spiritual assurance, may indicate remarkable exaltation of mind, but it is accompanied with a remarkable disagreeableness of temper. The habit of looking on one's opponents as liars is conducive neither to goodness nor to truth. Till dogma becomes pretty well formed, it is never done ; but after it has become pretty well formed, it is always done. The first Christians regarded all faiths save their own, especially what they called Gentile faiths, what we know to have been the faiths of the keenest minds of their age, as inspirations of the devil. A legend of St. John relates that, on one occasion, seeing Cerinthus, a noted heretic, enter a public bath, he warned the inmates to flee for their lives, for the building would surely fall on the false pretender. Thirty years ago, Mahomet was always called the "Impostor." He still is called so by zealous Chris-

tian writers. In the generations immediately sub-
sequent to his career, the Arabian prophet was
held in horror by the Church as the "Adversary,"
the father of lies himself. He was cursed as a
false god, to whom human sacrifices were offered.
Our ugly words, " buffoonery " and " mummery "
are supposed to derive from the nicknames given
to him. Three hundred years elapsed before he
was honored with so harmless a name as false
prophet, impostor, heresiarch. It was magnani-
mous in Dante to assign him an honorable place
in hell among the great sowers of discord. Or-
cagna, a celebrated painter who lived nearly a
century later, introduced him into his picture of
Hell on the wall of the Pisan Campo Santo,
along with Averroës and the antichrist, the
three roasting in flames, as despisers of all religion. In the middle ages, Mahomet was regarded as a sorcerer, a debauched wretch, a thief,
a spiteful cardinal who invented a new religion
in order to avenge himself on his colleagues who
would not make him pope. There was no limit
to the abuse that was heaped on the prophet's
name; and all because he was not a Christian.
He was no believer, therefore he was a liar.

The Romish missionaries in India finding
there a religion in many respects resembling their
own, were confident that the devil was trying to
baffle them by a counterfeit of the true faith.
Here were fine spiritualities, noble moralities, lofty

worships which owned no indebtedness to their church. Of course they were delusions of Satan. Had the Buddhist worshippers called themselves Christians, their beliefs would have been welcomed as inspirations from above ; as they did not call themselves so they were denounced as instigations from below. Their beauty was their bane.

It is the fashion to speak of the religions of the East as tissues of error and superstition, their good points being concealed, their bad points being magnified ; their truth being qualified, their error being exaggerated. The zealous Protestant polemic still denounces the Church of Rome as a mass of imposition. Its priests are hypocrites, its theologians are dishonest attorneys, its teachers are abettors of fraud, its devotees are either dupes or knaves. The furious "liberal" cannot allow sincerity to the preachers of trinity, deity of Christ, vicarious atonement, depravity, eternal perdition. Honest men, they think, cannot believe such nonsense. They must be either deceived or deceivers. And the judgment is handed down from sect to sect. Error is antichrist ; and everything is error which we do not assent to. Infallibility is the claim of each petty sectary, and infallibility will put hundreds under the ban. Strange, that people should be content with uncertainty where uncertainty is both needless and dangerous, and should demand certainty where certainty is neither possible nor wise. But

so it is. Thousands are satisfied not to know
their own minds who are indignant at being supposed unacquainted with the inmost mind of God.
They know nothing and are happy in knowing
nothing respecting the constitution of society, the
laws of government, or the proper regulation of
families, but the secret administration of the universe is familiar to them as their nursery rhymes.
Why their neighbors or their neighbors' children
behave as they do, is a mystery they despair of
solving, though a moment's reflection would solve
it; but why the Almighty does as He does is
plain. Of practical information regarding things
of hourly importance they possess and seek to acquire little; but the ultimate causes of things are
revealed, and the supreme First Cause they are
shocked to find any hesitating about. It does
not trouble them to be in the dark as to the issues
of to-morrow, but they are in agonies of despair
if the least misgiving cross their minds as to the
condition of the soul after death. Is this an evidence of the greatness of their being, their affi-
nity with divine things, the firmness of their
hold on eternal realities, the upspringing force
of their spiritual nature? or is it a proof of mental dreaminess? or is it a habit of intellectual
pride and stubbornness? Whether it be one of
these, or all, or neither, it has led to sad misinter-
pretations of thought, and melancholy injustice to
thinkers.

Here, for instance, is the general and severe condemnation of doubt which we have heard from our infancy, and hear on all sides now. Beware of doubt, is the warning given to young and old. Wrestle with it, pray against it, avoid it, turn the mind in other directions, fortify yourself against its assaults, shun all who question, cultivate the society of such as implicitly believe. Tennyson is thought to have said a very strong thing when he penned the lines :

> " There lives more faith in honest doubt,
> Believe me, than in half your creeds."

Of course there does. In *honest* doubt there lives more faith than in all the creeds. In *honest* doubt is all the live faith that exists. The creeds express the satisfied doubt of past ages. The doubts contain the possible creed of ages to come. All beliefs came from doubt. Christianity was born of doubt ; Romanism was born of doubt ; Protestantism was born of doubt ; Universalism and Unitarianism were born of doubt ; Science was born of doubt ; literatures, arts, economics, theories of government, principles of reform, schemes of education, are born of doubt. The spirit of truth manifests itself in the form of doubt. In doubt, the intellectual faculties are seen pressing beyond the lines of acquired knowledge into the realm of unexplored truth. Doubt is the evidence of live mind. The creeds mark

the point which mind has reached and where
mind rests. Doubt is the tingling of new vitality in the brain, the movement of fresh waves of
spiritual power.

Fairly understood, all mind is live mind. Mind
is vital. Immobile mind has ceased to be mind.
Intellect, in its normal action, is creative, not
destructive ; it ever builds, it never pulls down.
The child's passion to break in pieces its pretty
toy used to be quoted as an evidence of the depravity of its nature ; it is now regarded as a
sign of awakening intelligence ; it wants to know
why its doll cries, why its lamb or horse moves
when wound up. The larger child wants to know
why the sacraments are deemed sacred ; why the
Bible has lived so long ; what makes people revere as they do priests and holy buildings. He
desires to know how the skies are supported,
and pulls down the scaffolding of Ptolemy to find
out. He desires to know what the earth is made
of, and sweeps off the rubbish of tradition in order to get at it. He desires to know what the
soul of man, of which so much has been said,
really is, and he waives off the priests that forbid his laying hands on it.

This is our attitude ; it is an attitude of entire faith. We believe that there is a soul of
goodness in things evil ; we believe that there is
a soul of truth in things erroneous. We believe that since the mind of man has been

awake, it has been seeking light, has abhorred darkness, has worked its way steadily and by the power of an inherent instinct towards a true solution of the problem of its destiny, has incessantly raised questions, and has tried passionately to find answers to them. We believe something more than that all error contains some particle of truth ; we believe that all error embodies a soul of truth ; that it was born of a wish to discover the truth, and owes whatever hold on mankind it has, to its success in giving to the spirit of truth a temporary form. We believe that the most hideous beliefs were an effort on the part of their makers to state some fact or indicate some law ; and the more hideous the doctrine, the more pathetic the story of the mind out of whose experience it came. Nor will it be difficult by-and-by, as knowledge matures, to lay bare the intellectual motives that have sprung the strange faiths of men into being. Let me by a few common examples illustrate the method and the certainty of this process.

The Unitarians regard the dogma of Trinity as a plain, palpable, self-evident error. A person, they say, cannot at the same instant be three persons and one person. The trinity excludes the unity, the unity excludes the trinity. The doctrine is a mathematical puzzle, held in defiance of reason, in spite of scripture, even against the demand of spiritual faith, and is defended by a perverse ingenuity that is resolute at all hazards to make out a case ; as the keystone of a theological system, it must be justified, and the holders of the system do their best to justify it ; but its only supports are sectarian obstinacy and sectarian ingenuity. Thus reasons the monotheistic Unitarian, failing to perceive that the doctrine of trinity was intended to establish the proper personality of God. The doctrine historically apprehended was apparently an attempt to state the belief that God was in the world and at the same time out of it, that the universe was divine, but did not exhaust the divine, that there was an essential unity in the whole creation, a complete accord between the creation and the creator, but that the two were not confounded. The Father represented the infinite, endless, unexhausted, inexhaustible capacities of Deity. The Son represented the organized and organizing power that expended itself in creation. The Spirit represented the continuous movement of power, the ceaseless intercourse, the perpetual action and reaction between the two. The doctrine was an attempt to reconcile theism with pantheism, unity with diversity, the Semitic with the Aryan principle. Its purpose was therefore to establish, not to weaken the divine personality. Call it a rude device, but no better has been yet discovered by theology.

Unitarians again regard as an error the doctrine of the deity of Christ. That one should be at once God and man seems to them a contradiction in terms; if man then not God; if God then not man; infinite or finite, one or the other; to be both at once is out of the question. God and man are, says the Unitarian, the opposite poles, the extreme terms of thought. God cannot compress himself within the limits of a human form; no human form will hold the spiritual contents of God. The doctrine originated in error, has been maintained by error, and is held in the spirit of dogmatism which is the spirit of error. It is possibly a repetition of the oriental fancies about incarnation which stole into the West by way of Alexandria, and was adopted along with the doctrine of angels and demons and other wild imaginations of the East. The ordinary Unitarian finds difficulty in believing that honest minds can entertain an opinion so repugnant to enlightened common sense. But if we look deeper we perceive that the early believers felt an essential identity of their nature and the divine. They felt as religious men have always felt, as devout minds feel now, that there was a point where the divine and the human met and mingled; that when God expressed himself perfectly, it must be in the form of humanity; that when man rose to his full spiritual stature he took on heavenly attributes. They were conscious of a divinity within them; they were compelled to think of divinity as having a human heart in its bosom. Are not finest qualities equally characteristic of the human and the divine ? The love of purity and truth, reverence for justice, sympathy, compassion, the soul of holiness, the heart of pity, are they not common to both ? God is most godlike when he shows justice, compassion, forgiveness. Man is most manlike when he exhibits the same. In love of that beneath them both are greatest. In moments of exaltation pious souls seemed to lose the sense of limitation in the absorbing nearness of the supreme being ; in their hours of humility they seemed to float on the bosom of the boundless sea ; in their moments of aspiration they launched out on a sea of light. God was all in all. This consciousness of intimacy between man and deity, struggles after expression in the doctrine of the deity of Christ. The typical man was God. The revealed God was ideal man. Too modest to affirm this truth of all mankind, too timid to claim it for any but the very best, the Christians confined the privilege to one, but that one stood for all, vindicated the truth for all, was the symbol to which all could look, the demonstration to which all could appeal. The statement it conveyed was clumsy and is obsolete ; but the truth is one of the grandest ever entertained by mankind.

The doctrine of Eden and the fall of Adam from a perfect estate is now considered an error well nigh exploded. We are assured by naturalists that the whole story of Eden is a fancy. The first earth, we are told authoritatively, was a wilderness, not a garden. How could there be a garden without a gardener? How could there be a garden without horticultural skill and taste? The garden and the happy people in it will come by and by through scientific cultivation and the arts of civilized man. The wilderness has not blossomed yet.

It is getting to be a commonplace now to say that the narrative in Genesis is an allegory; and if it is, what then? May not an allegory convey a truth, or at least, an effort to reach a truth? The doctrine of Eden and the Fall was an endeavor to put into words the feeling that a state of poverty, want, misery, conflict, is not the normal state of man; that the normal state of man is one of innocence, contentment and peace; that man is not truly himself when a slave to his animal wants, the creature of his circumstances, degraded by fears and crushed by sorrows; but that man is truly himself when free from toil and care, upright, calm and happy. The vision of a golden age and a perfect manhood hovered therefore before earnest minds. They could not anticipate it in the future; that required more vigor and hopefulness than they possessed, more command of their circumstances, more assurance of progress; and so they did the only thing they could, they pictured it in the past as a memory.

They looked backward as we look towards our childhood and imagine heaven as lying about our infancy. We call it an error, and so I believe it was and always is. Childhoods were never so blissful as old folks imagine. Children are not so much happier than men and women are, and such happiness as they have is childish. The golden age is yet to dawn. We dream of the good time coming, as the children of the race dreamed of the good time gone. The dreams differ. Ours is the more hopeful, theirs is the more pensive. Ours is the dream of expectancy; theirs was the dream of regret. Ours is the dream of courage; theirs was the dream of fatigue. Ours is a dream of conquest; theirs was a dream of defeat. But both dream, and the dreamer in either case is a being haunted by the notion that a state of poverty, want, misery and struggle is not his normal state.

Is any error more apparent than the doctrine of total depravity? It declares that, our first parents sinned in eating the forbidden fruit. They being the root of all mankind the guilt of this sin was imitated and the same death in sin and corrupted nature conveyed to all their posterity. This is horrible. But did the first conceivers of it rejoice in the dismal view of humanity they were holding? Did they deliberately choose to entertain such ideas of themselves? Were they cynics or misanthropes?

Did they think this the worst possible world? Did the spirit of mischief and deceit possess them and compel a faith so abhorrent to all conceptions of equity and so opposed to the testimony of human experience? That can hardly be. They must have had something in their minds that struggled for voice. What was it, but the fact that man is limited, constrained, incapable, imbecile, that he cannot at the moment do what he would, cannot break his bonds, restrain his passions, eradicate his vices, put away his infirmites, lift off the burden of his social evils, make himself and the world in an instant just what they should be? What is it but the fact so intimately connected with this, so closely a part of this, that the men of the one generation inherit from the generations that have gone before, and that this inheritance is largely one of pain, weakness, and sorrow? This is a fact we cannot deny or overlook, or banish from memory. It stares us in the face every hour. It is more palpable, more appalling in magnitude, more organically knit to the texture of things than our remote ancestors could perceive, only they, as it seems, dwelt more upon it, were more staggered by it, and wrestled more fiercely with it than we. How they wrestled with it, appears in this strange, uncouth dogma that the first man in falling from his high estate dragged after him the whole line of his descendants, planting in them the seeds of deadly desires, and committing them ages in advance to disobedience, crime, and guilt. It is a problem that we have not fully solved yet. We have given new names to the facts, calling them crudeness and imperfection, but we have not altered them. We have set the law of transmission in a new light, regarding it as a principle of progress instead of re-trogression, but we have not annulled it. Our solution is wiser, but the problem remains as it was, nor is our determination to vanquish it a whit more earnest than was that of the elders. Our search, if more successful, is no more resolute or keen.

The doctrine of election presents a hateful aspect to the modern mind. How was it possible, we ask, for men to believe that God picked out a certain number of people for blessedness and a certain number for misery, without the smallest reference to character or merit on their part, without explanation or apology on his own, but simply because, in his inscrutable and arbitrary purpose, he saw fit to do so? loving Jacob and hating Esau, though Esau was every whit as deserving as Jacob, and, according to the human view, worthier of esteem, and extending that love that hatred to generations of men and women, never giving them the option of their birth, or offering them a

chance to alter their destiny? The doctrine
as presented in the Protestant confessions outrages every sentiment of the heart and every
principle of reason. But here too we may easily discover the effort of sincere minds to get
some light on the most mysterious questions
that existence presses on attention. Even
thoughtless persons are startled sometimes by
strange freaks of destiny, signs of arbitrary ca-
price in mortal affairs, the action as of some
occult principle that makes naught of justice.
They call it "luck," "chance," "misfortune,"
and there leave it. But earnest intellects cannot leave it there; the arbitrary element in fate
bewilders and appalls them. They see, as it were,
some demon playing with God's dice, and en-
joying the sport. One race is born to perpetual servitude, another to perpetual mastery.
One tribe is set in the very front rank of progress, favored by all winds, lighted by all the
constellations, sunned by all the heavenly orbs,
another is placed far in the rear, buried in
deep valleys, sunk in morasses, held in thrall-
dom by nature, with no opportunity of convert-
ing a single element to friendly uses. One
child is born physically perfect, and grows up
to the fullest use of its powers in a world of
beauty, delight and privilege; another comes into
life a cripple, and is doomed to suffering, disa-

bility, wretchedness in a world where everything hurts and hinders.

One is born to wealth and social position, and
all that we mean by advantage. Gifted, his powers are enriched by travel and commerce with the
opulent minds of his own and other ages; ungifted, his ordinariness is covered up by position,
or atoned for by joy. Another is born to poverty,
obscurity, and deprivation. Gifted, his powers
run to waste from want of culture, or torment
their possessor with hopeless dreams of unattain-
able fame; ungifted, he gets no taste of the
world's bounty—not so much as a glimpse at its
glory. One is born amid circumstances discouraging to worthy effort, amid people of vicious
character and life; another is welcomed to precepts of virtue and examples of excellence. More
perplexing and staggering to the ordinary mind
is the familiar fact that some inherit tendencies to
goodness from their parents, they hunger after
righteousness, principles of truth and honesty, as-
·pirations toward the pure and saintly life, are
destined as it were to be exemplars of excellence,
benefactors of their fellows, beloved and honored;
while some of the same social rank, perhaps off-
spring of parents equally virtuous and careful,
possibly of the same parents, suck up from the
blood of a remote ancestor the black drop of
moral disease, the low appetite, the base lust, the
mania for theft or murder; and, unwilling, writh-

ing victims, often, of guilt not their own, become a weariness to themselves, a curse to their families, a nuisance to society, and a disgrace to their kind.

These are frightful facts, open to all men's observation. They hint at a mysterious law of election, operating in circumstance and inherited disposition, the track whereof has never been traced. We are unable to explain these things ; we cannot account for them scientifically, or work them into a philosophical scheme of the world, or reconcile them with the rule of a just and merciful God. The rational solution of them is abandoned by the mass of mankind, who have neither the feeling nor the intelligence to grapple with questions so appalling. The minds that started the doctrine of election could not lose them from view, or forget them, or give over the attempt to explain and justify them. Their method was simple and rude, not at all nice, delicate, or scientific. They cut the knot they were unable to untie, and failing to dig the heart out of the mystery, bowed their own hearts beneath it. Their recourse was artless. Finding the facts unmanageable, they just collected the whole shocking mass of facts together, and flung it upon the broad shoulders of the upholder of the universe. Let the responsibility rest there, with the supremely just and wise ; and let men stand with bended head before the inscrutable will that can no more be questioned or challenged than it can be altered. If these humble theologians exhibited no wonderful genius for philosophy, they exhibited a wonderful power of trust, an awful confidence in the Almighty, which proved them possessed, if not of cunning brains, still of indomitable hearts.

Let us now approach in the same spirit that most horrible of all beliefs ever invented or entertained by men, the belief in an eternity of torture for the wicked. ـ For the last fifty years and more the belief has been dying out of the actively professed credence of Christendom, and is now virtually discarded by intelligent evangelical minds. In the extreme form under which it was preached by Jonathan Edwards and divines of his school in the last century and stated in church catechisms, it is frankly pronounced an error. Conscience protests against it in the name of outraged justice; the heart cries out against it in the name of pity; philosophy hoots at it in the name of reason; judgment refuses to listen to it in the name of common sense. It is customary in our days to accuse those who bring it up to the discredit of Calvinism, of willful exaggeration. The charge is just only as applied to modern believers. It is impossible to overstate the hideousness of the doctrine as presented by authorized creeds, and defended once by famous teachers. What then? Was it an inspiration of the devil, a

suggestion of Satan, a lie of the arch deceiver?
Did the men who invented it purpose to insult
the deity, or to bring the divine order into disrepute? Were they savages with hearts full of
malignity, or fiends, who exulted in the thought
of millions of human creatures groaning in intolerable torments for ages without end? The
mind refuses to entertain such a wild idea.
They were men, as anxious as we are, more
anxious than we are probably, to pluck out the
moral secrets of Providence, men who loved
children and friends, and wished to repose in
faith on the holy kindness of the eternal. They
were no more heartless or cruel than the best
of us, *but they were more deeply impressed with
the hatefulness of guilt than we are.* They were
more in the habit than we are of measuring
guilt by supreme standards, judging it by absolute laws, setting it in the light of the Christ's
clear eye, and contemplating it as an affront
on the serene majesty of heaven. The world to
them was poor and small; life was short and
fleeting; existence was not in itself a boon;
they were accustomed to pain, suffering, the tyranny of despotic powers; their temporal goods
were precarious; their secular relations were incidental. *They lived in their souls.* The divine
holiness and sweetness, the inestimable gift of
a saviour, the unmerited graciousness of the
Son of God in giving himself up as a sacrifice

for the sins of mankind, the amazing promises
of peace here and bliss hereafter held out by
the church to the meanest of mankind, the un-
purchased, unpurchasable glory.of an unending
heaven were subjects of unceasing meditation.
And as meditation brought them home, the utter ingratitude and turpitude of the vicious
and wicked seemed too abominable to deserve
the least consideration. Simple justice pronounced the sternest doom. They belonged
among the fiends, and were even lower than
the fiends as having sinned against a more
amazing goodness. They were chaff fit only to
be thrown into the fire and burned ; unfortunately, being made of spiritual stuff they must
burn forever. As Draco, the Athenian lawgiv-
er, when asked why, in his code, he fixed but
one penalty,—death—to all grades of offence,
replied, because the smallest crime merits death,
and there is no severer punishment for the
greatest, so these fanatics for God's righteousness included all transgressors in the same verdict of holy wrath.

And had they no encouragement to do this,
in the fearful law of compensation which they
saw as clearly as we do and comprehended as
little, a law that brings down on every fault
and foible a .weight of penalty out of all proportion apparently to the transgression ? The
sweep of this awful law that looks anything

but kind and pitiful to our eyes, had early made an impression on the minds of sensitive men, and crowded their imaginations with images of fear. The ancient books of the East, Indian, Persian, Egyptian, Hebrew, Greek, are full of it, and in those books the master minds of theology were nurtured.

It was not strange that, in a less sentimental age than ours, the doctrine of endless torment for the wicked should have grown out of all this observation and all this experience. Least of all is it strange that it should have been shaped into complete form by the holiest, purest, sweetest and devoutest souls. It was the way the saints had of interpreting the counsels and vindicating the sanctity of God. If any souls were ever inspired by a loyal love of the truth, theirs were. That a man like Jonathan Edwards could have written and preached his frightful sermon, "Sinners in the hand of an angry God," so divine a person proclaiming so devilish a message, is one of the marvels of psychology. But that he did it, is proof that in this dreary and now widely repudiated error there was a soul of truth. The sooner the grotesque error perishes, the better for all men. It will perish the sooner as the soul of truth in it is encouraged to reconstruct opinion on rational grounds.

And if, in such hateful forms of error as these,

the soul of truth is discernible, it should be possible to discover it under modern forms of error, which we deplore. Materialism we regard as an error, and a dreadful one ; a fatally one-sided statement of the case it deals with, cheerless to the heart, darkening to the mind, discouraging to the soul. But Materialism is, at bottom, a well-meant endeavor to render justice to the organization, hitherto neglected. It wishes to give to organized matter its dues, and if in this noble endeavor it overreaches its point, and makes organization everything, destroying and sinking the mentality of mind, this is the inevitable partiality of other systems. Few men see truth in all its aspects ; very few see it in its opposite aspects. Spiritualism is as one-sided as Materialism.

There is a soul of truth in Atheism. The Atheist wishes to vindicate the prerogative of natural law; to demonstrate the natural order, the perfect sequence and consistency of the world, the sufficiency of the universe as constituted for all the ends of its constitution, the needlessness of interference with established conditions, the full *enworlding,* so to speak, of the creative mind. Hence his antipathy to the popular conceptions of God as a being of special plans and purposes, a God who must needs arrange and rearrange the running machinery of creation, who can be moved by prayer, or who must resort to occasional expedients to prevent catastrophe to his projects. What is called God, says the Atheist, I know not. He is beyond my reach and ken. Law I believe in, and Beauty, and Order, and Justice, and Goodness. Creation teaches me these ; the ideals of them stand continually before my thought. But what I am concerned that all shall know and be convinced of, is that the universe itself is a whole body of divinity, a compact, and to all practical purposes an infinite system of elements and powers, marvellously adjusted to each other, and fully capable of working out ends vast in scope and glorious in design. There is the soul of truth in the Atheist ; a soul great enough to excuse graver errors than he falls into, and to relieve his name from the reproach that heresy haters have fastened upon it.

A soul of truth in things erroneous. Surely there is one, " would men observingly distill it out." To do this gracious work will be the task of many minds for many years. But the task is begun ; it has already proceeded far, and the results of it are felt in more hopeful views of man's ultimate destiny. It is a glorious thing to believe that a soul of truth has from the beginning been active in the race ; that while error abounds, while in fact nothing but error exists, since truth is but partial, in another sense nothing but truth exists, since error testifies to the presence of truth, is indeed but truth in the making. To believe that the mind of man is ever pushing towards light, though it may never reach its source. To be sure that while " our little systems have their day," they cease to be, only because their " broken lights" must give way to clearer senses, such a belief makes all systems positive, all creeds respectable, all confessions honorable. It abolishes enmity between schools ; it suggests a brotherhood of believers ; it brings East and West and North and South together in bonds of peace ; makes voices formerly discordant and quarrelsome ring in unison ; and proclaims aloud the symphonies of faith. The symphonies of faith, I say, not the indifference of creeds ; the identity of the thinking principle, not the equal value of its results. It is the soul of truth that is venerable, not the thing erroneous ; the questioning mind, not the incoherent answer. The beliefs are arrested thoughts, let them go ; the thought that cannot be arrested, let that pass on.

The old polemics stand henceforth rebuked. To the bloody strife in the arena of theology will succeed the emulous race on the course of truth. The business of *fighting* error by denying the soul of truth in it is over. The business of supplanting error by new force of the soul that made it, is started. The errors are dismissed by their own more enlightened author. They only are to be condemned who perpetuate the error *because it was true once.* These are the antichrists, the ene-

mies of faith ; these having lost sight of the soul
of truth, are entitled to no consideration. They
hold error in the spirit of error. Fight *that spirit*,
and the error will disappear. Theological hatred
should cease. Ephraim shall not envy Judah,
and Judah shall not vex Ephraim. The sincere
Protestant should not malign Romanism, nor
the thoughtful Romanist curse Protestantism.
Calvin should no longer be a name abhorred by
Universalists, nor Athanasius be a name dreaded
by Unitarians. Rationalists will no longer put
the worst interpretations on the creeds they have
discarded, or denounce as barren superstitions
the grim texts of a by-gone day. Sacred writings will be read with more discerning, because
more reverent eyes ; justice will be done to ancient myths, symbols, and monuments which have
ceased to be intelligible. It will not be considered honest or decent to deal in the spirit of
caricature with phrases or dogmas that seem to
modern apprehension outlandish or grotesque.
All forms of error, however strange, will be regarded with tender respect, as painful endeavors
after the truth ; and no forms of truth, however
fair to the eye, will be honored with more respect than is due to equally well meant endeavors in the same direction. There will be no
more intellectual superciliousness or spiritual
contempt, no more assumption of infallibility, no

more claim to authority, no more conceit of final discovery. With mingled pride and humility, earnest minds will address themselves to their task of·enlightening themselves and mankind; pride, as they look back and see how nobly intelligence has faced the terrible problems of being; humility, as they look forward and see how feeble their own efforts are. The great prayer will be for the Spirit of Truth, that shall lead them a little way further towards all truth.

THE END.

www.ingramcontent.com/pod-product-compliance
Lightning Source LLC
Chambersburg PA
CBHW020933030726
47496CB00005B/1165